The Hidden Side of the Mountain

The Hidden Side of the Mountain

Encounters with
Wisdom's Poor and Holy

by Deacon Lucien Miller

FONS VITAE

First published in 2021 by
Fons Vitae
49 Mockingbird Valley Drive
Louisville, KY 40207
http://www.fonsvitae.com
Email: fonsvitaeky@aol.com

ISBN 978-194610-824

Printed in USA

Contents

Dedication

To Bonnie

Three Strokes
Bonnie Miller

Preface
The Invisible Side of Mountains

Guided by writer and Trappist monk, Thomas Merton (1915-1968), and his end of life journey to the East, I found myself throughout my life on pilgrimages, stumbling upon the hapless poor in China and India, and discovering my self and vocation beyond words to tell them. In Sri Lanka (Ceylon), again due to Merton, I was led to the discovery of Buddhist Asia's *Hagia* Sophia, Holy Wisdom, the mystical reality which I believe underlies religious faiths and human reason. Like Thomas Merton, while he was on retreat in the Himalayas in the final days of his life, gazing upon Mount Kanchenjunga, I too chanced upon the other side of the mountain which has never been seen or photographed.[1] Simultaneously, as I resided in India and China, I encountered the sides of mountains that have been seen and photographed endlessly, the world of the pure of heart and the lowly poor whom I beheld in a bafflingly mysterious light.[2]

The other side of the Mountain that Merton saw and then recorded in his journal a week before his death on December 10, 1968, near Bangkok, Thailand, is well known and widely celebrated. In the twelfth century Sinhalese Buddhist vale of Gal Vihara at Polonnaruwa, Sri Lanka, as he faced the rock relief statues of the Buddha carved into the granite walls, Merton experienced a vision of the Buddhist Other.

> The path dips down to Gal Vihara: a wide, quiet, hollow, surrounded with trees. A low outcrop of rock, with a cave cut into it, and beside the cave . . . a reclining Buddha on the right, and Ananda, I guess, [actually, Buddha] standing by the head of the reclining Buddha . . . . I am able to approach the Buddhas barefoot and undisturbed, my feet in wet grass, wet sand. Then the silence of the extraordinary faces. The great smiles. Huge and subtle. Filled with every possibility, questioning nothing, knowing everything, rejecting nothing . . . I was knocked over with a rush of relief and thankfulness at the *obvious* clarity of the figures, the clarity and fluidity of shape and line, the design of the monumental bodies composed into the rock shape and landscape, figure, rock and tree.
>
> . . . I don't know when in my life I have ever had such a sense of

beauty and spiritual validity running together in one aesthetic illumination . . . I know and have seen what I was obscurely looking for.[3]

When my wife and I visited Gal Vihara some thirty years after Merton's passage, I too heard a bell ringing from a mystical cathedral. The echo of its ringing had passed through Merton's ears, and it was now reverberating in my own.

Before he visited Polonnaruwa and the other side of Buddha's mountain, Merton had seen the side of the mountain of poverty that was all too visible. In Kolkata (Calcutta), Merton had toured the world of the Holy Innocents about whom he had written so passionately in his prophetic works of moral outrage and was now personally encountering. The Holy Innocents are those who suffer through no fault of their own—like the male babies under two years old King Herod ordered massacred out of his fear that the Christ Child might replace him (Matthew 2:16-18). These are the *anawim* (*inwetan*), the Hebrew word for the "poor ones," those bowed down. They are known in the Hebrew Bible (the textual source for the Christian Old Testament) as the powerless, the lowly, humble remnant of the faithful who are materially poor, yet remain devoted believers in God in times of affliction.[4] In an extended, spiritual sense, the Holy Innocents are the poorest of the poor—powerless and pitiful, rejected and persecuted, forgotten, and afflicted. Merton wrote of these as victims "for whom there is no room":[5]

> Calcutta is shocking because it is all of a sudden a totally different kind of madness . . . Calcutta has the lucidity of despair, of absolute confusion, of vitality helpless to cope with itself . . . An infinite crowd of men and women camping everywhere as if waiting for someone to lead them in an ultimate exodus into reasonableness . . . yet knowing already beyond contradiction that in the end, *nothing* really works.[6]

Merton's pilgrimage to Asia was deeply intentional, my own less so. The meanings of my journeys to Asia would gradually reveal themselves to me during my sabbaticals and research in China, Hong Kong, Taiwan, Japan, India, and Sri Lanka. I could signify my experiences as fate, circumstances, coincidences, and destiny. Now looking back over my life's eight decades, I realize that the mysteries of being on "pilgrimage" encapsulate my life. Pilgrimage is a mystery that moves mountains yet hovers over the briefest, by chance encounters with particular people in a specific time and place, with my being with them in singular circumstances. I was the stranger only passing through among these people belonging to an Asian spiritual faith and cultural tradition, who were members of an ethnic minority. Many whom I would meet were social outcasts in their own countries.

My stories here are spiritual parables with signs for me pointing to the mysterious, hidden sides of mountains, the shapes of things behind the visible mountains we cannot see, but dare surmise we comprehend. During my teaching sabbaticals, field trips, and vacations to East Asia, everything was palpably new—people, dialects, places, events. A hidden thread binding everything I encountered together emerged slowly, like a piece of woolen yarn that seemed to weave itself into an ancient oriental rug that enwrapped and enclosed me within an intensely human and spiritual vocation. I would learn my destiny by visiting the hidden side of Asia. I would slowly understand it was my life's best pilgrimage to search in East and Southeast Asia for my self guided by a divine providence that would bear me more securely to become a citizen in an unexpected, more invisible world.

Acknowledgements to: dear friends Fran Howe for her discerning guidance and Dan Robb for his presiding over and expert editing of earlier versions; my dear friend and colleague, Professor Chisato Kitagawa, without whose help and our contemplative breakfasts together my writing on Father Shigeto Oshida and things Japanese would have been impossible; his wife Mary Kitagawa whose kind close reading corrected a myriad of mistakes; Susan Solinsky whose literary acumen taught me to think and write better than I had imagined possible; my soulmate in Christ Anne Martens, artist, book designer, and photographer whose peerless cover, photography, and selfless guidance brought this volume to fruition; dear friend, former colleague, biographer, and poet Paul Mariani whose warm support inspired me; spiritual master, writer, editor, retreat and conference presenter Jonathan Montaldo whose ardor and editing "translation" made my book what it is; Gray Henry and Neville Blakmore of Fons Vitae publications for their care, expertise, and enthusiasm for my writing; my children Anita, Lucia, and Nick and grandson Nicholas for making my string of beads into a rosary; granddaughters Gillian and Allie, and grandsons Aidan, James, and Cameron for cheering me on; and most of all to Bonnie my beloved wife for her guiding light and love beyond all telling.

West Meets East
Abbot Thomas Keating and Joshu Sasaki Roshi at St. Joseph's Cistercian Abbey, Spencer, Massachusetts

Thomas Merton realized he could move more West by going East when he met by correspondence Dr. John C. H. Wu, a Professor of Chinese at Seton Hall University. They would eventually collaborate on Merton's *The Way of Chuang Tzu*. As Catholics and learned men, they convinced one another that the study of eastern philosophy sheds unrealized new light on their Christian belief. Asian thought would reveal the other side of the Gospels to meet another Christ.[7] In East Asian religions and philosophies, they intuited echos of the crib of straw in Bethlehem, the Sermon on the Mount, the Last Supper discourse, the Cross, and Resurrection.[8] My accidental encounter with Merton and Wu's Asian collaborative enlightenment would, in time, foster an epiphany for the deepening of my traditionalist Catholic faith.

While completing my first 1969-1970 academic year of teaching Comparative Literature and Chinese at the University of Massachusetts, Amherst, and inspired by Thomas Merton, I had proposed teaching a new undergraduate course, "Mystical Literature East and West" for the following fall. Instead, our department secretary unwittingly signed me up to offer the course in the preceding summer school, 1970. I had no idea at the time that contemplative literature courses would become a mainstay of my thirty-five years of teaching. Coincidentally, a high school teacher who enrolled in that first course's summer school meeting had a former colleague who was now a secretary at St. Joseph's Cistercian (Trappist) Abbey in Spencer, Massachusetts. Learning of my curiosity about monasticism and the contemplative life of monks, he took me to meet her. After our first meeting over tea, she dropped me at the monastery, where the Guest-Master gave me a tour. While walking through a corridor, he opened the door of an elderly monk's cell, and smiling pushed me gently inside and closed the door. Somehow, this senior monk, who was Father John Holohan, seemed to know me. To my complete surprise, he asked if I would be interested in bringing students to the Abbey to introduce them to monastic spirituality. With a twinkle in his rheumy eye, he said, "It might be helpful for their studies." I was immediately enthusiastic.

Abbot Thomas Keating OCSO
Photo Contemplative life.org

Joshu Sasaki Roshi
Photo Alois Payer

Early that September, I received a call from still another monk at Spencer Abbey. A Japanese Zen master, Joshu Sasaki Roshi, had just arrived at the monastery's doorstep. He only spoke a little English. Did I know someone who could serve as a bilingual translator—one who not only could translate Japanese but was also familiar with Buddhist philosophy and Christian theology? Abbot Thomas Keating had just begun his 1970s decade of reaching out to non-Christian religions in the spirit of the Vatican II Council (1962-1965). Keating wanted to have a formal luncheon the very next day with Sasaki Roshi to consider the possibility of inviting him to give talks on Zen Buddhism to any interested monks. So, I immediately began phoning colleges in our Five-College area, where I knew they offered Japanese in their Asian Studies programs. At Smith College, the very first institution I called, the person who picked up the phone was Professor Taitetsu Unno, a good friend of the Roshi, who had just arrived at Smith College to teach Buddhist studies and philosophy. "Ty" as his colleagues called him was a Buddhist priest as well who had long studied Christian history and theology. Early the next morning, Ty and I scurried to the Abbey to attend the first historic meeting between a Trappist abbot and a Buddhist roshi.

The high point of the Abbey luncheon came after a pleasant exchange of welcoming words following the meal. Very tall ascetic-looking Abbot Keating pushed back his chair and turned to his Far East spiritual counterpart, the very short, stout-framed, thick-necked Sasaki Roshi. Gazing at his long delicate fingers, Father Keating asked, "Well, Roshi, *if* we should invite you to our Abbey, *what* would you teach us?"

"I teach you Crucifixion and Resurrection," Roshi stated without a moment's hesitation. That was good enough for Abbot Keating.

Subsequently, during the 1970s, Sasaki Roshi came several times to St. Joseph's Abbey and Mary House across the street (an independently owned and operated lay retreat center for anyone wanting silence and solitude) to give week-long Zen Buddhist *sesshin*. I participated in these. It was the beginning of my introduction to Christian-Buddhist encounter and my thirty-five years of bringing students from the University of Massachusetts and the area's Five Colleges to Mary House for silent Catholic-Zen weekend retreats and an introduction to Trappist monastic spirituality.

Father William Johnston's Charismatic Zen
Taiwan, Republic of China

In the summer of 1976, I had ended a sabbatical in Taiwan with my family. The day before my departure, I saw a tattered announcement posted on a telephone pole. A week-long "Charismatic-Zen retreat" would begin the next day in Tanshui, north Taiwan. Father William Johnston, a gifted Irish Jesuit at Sophia University in Tokyo, was presenting the retreat.[9] The poster stated that Father Johnston felt the Catholic Church's encounter with Buddhist and other Asian contemplative traditions to be the work of the Holy Spirit, thus his choice of the word "charismatic" for the naming of his pioneering Christian-Buddhist retreats. I immediately called the Catholic convent and signed up to fill the last open space available. After seeing my wife Bonnie and the children off at the Taipei airport, I scampered to catch a taxi to Tanshui.

Being a late arrival, I rushed to open the heavy chapel doors, announcing with a mighty thud my presence to a full gathering of retreatants sitting silently in their pews. Suddenly, here I was the sole layman among a group of Catholic priests and sisters, most of them American-born who were serving as missionaries in Taiwan. I looked and felt like a lay misfit, especially since Father Johnston had to wait to begin the retreat because of me. As I dashed into a pew and looked up, I experienced a Catholic's shock. To my utter surprise, Father Johnston appeared in black Japanese yukata robes, instead of a priest's black suit. He bowed deeply before the altar, where he placed the Eucharist in a ciborium in plain view instead of in the tabernacle where it belonged. Turning to face us, he sat *zazen* style with his legs crossed on a Zen cushion with the ciborium behind his back. There was no "In the Name of the Father" or "let us pray." We simply maintained a long silence. Many of the religious women and men retreatants were wearing dressing gowns or robes, while the priests among them had on cassocks. Everyone but me had dressed appropriately for a Zen *sesshin.* I guessed many were fellow neophytes like me as we all awkwardly sat *zazen* with legs crossed as best we could. We would quickly discover together that, for the uninitiated Westerner, *zazen* would initially prove a painful affair.

Johnston's presentation was that of an oral story-teller, intimate and

William Johnston, S.J.
Photo Source Unknown

dynamic, his voice a felt bodily presence. We experienced a living relationship between himself and us, an intimacy that carried in his voice. It was warm, friendly, and penetrating, and he spoke in a smoothly flowing, natural rhythm, with an appealing immediacy which made us eager to hear and understand. His words came spontaneously, passionately, from deep within.

Much to our surprise, he insisted, "Sitting is not central. What is central is faith. [Chinese 'shin' 信, a person 人 standing beside his word 言.] The Buddhists say the same thing. You do not hear much about this in western books on Buddhism, but you have to have the faith as a Buddhist that you will be enlightened. Christians have to believe that God loves them. Buddhists believe that everything is all right; there is no need to worry. For the Christian, there comes a time when an existential experience happens—the individual truly realizes that *'everything is all right.'* The key is an attitude of mind—Faith: I can achieve a breakthrough. We can enter into contemplation. Having faith is a liberation from fear." Decades later, I would awaken to Pope Francis' mature sense of faith: "Faith is a bond with God that engages the whole person."[10]

During a private talk, I met with Father Johnston in a spacious outdoor alcove adjacent to his room, overlooking an exquisite natural Japanese garden with a fishpond replete with multi-colored koi. The fragrance of some late-blooming flower hovered in the air. "Christian-Zen has a great future, and Christians need and want it," he affirmed. "Experience is the very best level of exchange," he reminded me, speaking broadly and succinctly. "When

Christians and Buddhists sit together, they are sharing something."

I explained to Johnston, in my experience of teaching world religions, I had encountered what I called "New England scar tissue." When I first began teaching contemplative literature of the East & West at Amherst, I gave the course's title as "Mystical Literature East & West." I soon roused my colleagues against yet another 1970s pop-culture and New Age production. So I decided upon the more formal "Readings in Buddhist, Taoist, Jewish, and Christian Teachings on Ultimate Reality." The faculty seemed slightly less wounded. Then I began to notice the students' responses whenever I spoke on the Judeo-Christian readings. When I said Asian words like "Buddha" or "Tao," students seemed tranquil and happy. The words "Bible" or "the New Testament" brought out a twitch or two. When I spoke about "Yahweh" or "God," they squirmed. And when I dared bring up "sin" as in Dante's *Inferno,* nearly everybody writhed, especially the Roman Catholics and the ex-Roman Catholics. It was as if Catholics were shouting, "Stop! Please stop, Professor Miller! You're killing us!" I was exposing their scar tissue from a negative Catholic religious past. Sometimes Protestants and Jews wiggled too.

This New England phenomenon was unknown to me, a native Californian. On the West Coast, ethnic and religious differences were often blurred, like the line between the Italian and Chinese districts in San Francisco. What set off students "out West" during the 1960s and 1970s, especially at UC Berkeley, were words like "J. Edgar Hoover," "House Un-American Activities Committee," and "the draft." On both coasts as I well knew, "spiritual but not religious" was generally OK.

Father Johnston was amused. "It's the seventies!" he laughed. He shared with me his view that students he taught were shifting their perspectives from West to East. It was unusual for those who became interested in Buddhism to remain Catholic.

His generalization startled me because the reverse was true to my experience. Resonating with Thomas Merton's grounding, Asian religions had deepened my Christian faith. Asian philosophy and culture allowed me to more deeply understand and personally rediscover my Catholic identity, interiority, and even Christianity's formal beliefs.

At the end of the Charismatic-Zen retreat, I met privately with Father Johnston one last time. Did he have any recommendations for me as to what I should do—what should I read?—the professorial element in my teaching brain still hard at work. How should I continue *zazen* practice? Did he think Zen had a future in the American Catholic church? He instantly made a suggestion that struck a chord deep within my being.

"If you are serious about encountering Buddhism and 'Christian Zen,'" he insisted, "you must go to Japan and meet Father Shigeto Oshida and stay with his Takamori Soan community."

Immediately a "Yes" flashed through my mind. I had a plane reservation leaving in two days for the States with a layover in Japan. A visa to stay in Japan was impossible on such short notice, but without any doubts, I decided that when my flight from Taipei to San Francisco landed at Haneda airport in Tokyo, I would jump ship. Feeling touched by the Spirit, I bid adieu to the happily swimming koi in the pond. Something deep within me was drawing me to Oshida. I was taking another step on a path I had never envisioned as my own. I have found the journey to which I am remaining faithful until I meet my destined end.[11]

Father Shigeto Oshida OP
The Buddhist Who Encountered Christ
Takamori Hermitage, Japanese Alps

Alone and without a visa, I made my visit to the Takamori Hermitage (Soan) and contemplative community in the Japan Alps above Nagano, founded by Father Shigeto Oshida, who titled himself "a Buddhist who encountered Christ."

With my first glimpse of Takamori, I felt I had dropped from the sky into an antique Japanese paradise: a handful of small cottages amidst the woods built in a traditional Japanese farmhouse style with thick thatched roofs, an adjacent rice field of golden stalks rustling in the breeze, and Koizumi, a crystal-clear spring-fed creek bubbling by, the scene of baptisms and prayer vigils. As I walked about, I saw everything suffused in an atmosphere of silence, poverty, harmony, and aesthetic beauty—Japanese *Wabi-Sabi*.

Hidden amidst deciduous trees and shrubbery was a small, exquisite building, the chapel (*Omido*). I felt its built-in harmony. All its elements shone with a beauty from an inner light: the reed window, the black luster of the walls from countless fires set in an iron pot during the offering of the Eucharist, the carpet woven from straw, the altar on the floor made from a single wooden plank, the altar cloth woven by a Takamori Sister, the kiln-fired pottery chalice, and the tabernacle made from a hollowed-out log affixed vertically to the chapel wall, with a pine door and a small pine box inside to house the Blessed Sacrament.

Takamori-Oshida
Photos from Japanese Dominican Archives

Omido

A Memorial Wood nearby was dedicated to victims of Japan's aggression during World War II and its warmongering throughout East Asia. Trees were inscribed with poems by Father Oshida memorializing "murdered" holy innocents "forgotten by the hidden Japanese conscience in the silence of the statesmen" [Father Oshida's words]. One of the memorial monuments honored the atomic bomb victims in Hiroshima and Nagasaki killed (or is it "murdered"?) by us Americans.

Having himself served in an anti-aircraft unit in Japan during the war, Father Oshida commented that his final poem in the center of the Memorial was his message of hope and encouragement to victims of atrocities, survivors of holocausts around the world, and the pilgrims to Takamori.

限りなき　なみだの海に　消えず　立たなむ　茂人
"Kagiri naki namida no umi ni kiezu tatanamu"

We shall stand with the disappearing
in the sea of infinite tears

Father Oshida's last poem points beyond Japan's sorrow to our guilt and forgetfulness as Americans to what we have done, to our need to pray *in memoriam* for the Holy Innocents we have destroyed through slavery, genocide, war, and abortion. We must stand fast in solidarity with the guiltless victims. We must confess our guilt and mourn their loss, resist war and iniquity, feed the hungry and shelter the poor, and never give up remembering the Holy Innocents, "lest we forget" (Deut. 4: 8-9) and repeat our evil, maiming, and destroying.

When I first entered Father Oshida's living quarters, a simple hut hidden in surrounding woods, I felt the glow of imperfection and impermanence, *wabi-sabi* again: rough walls made of unfinished planks, a feeling of austerity and the intimacy of natural objects, papers piled on a desk, books here and there in no particular order. Looking through a series of small doorless spaces, I saw Father Oshida sitting behind his desk, burrowed away far in the back, as he was leafing through a beautiful Japanese manuscript hand-written in classical Japanese.

Father Shigeto Oshida OP

Gazing up and seeing me from afar, he saw me approach his desk, a look of serenity on his bemused face, as I awkwardly moved my big body forward, bumping against various objects, a chair or two, and through a narrow passageway. He had a kind look, though rather drawn, it seemed, as though he were somewhat worn down by being a hermit in community, a host for years to too many thousands of foreign visitors from around the world and their concerns. With a bit of a giggle, he rose, came forward, smiled graciously, and opened his arms wide in greeting. Gesturing to two hard stuffed pillows before his desk, he invited me to sit down. I noticed he was holding the note I had air-mailed in haste to him before leaving Taiwan, asking if I could visit.

"So, what brings you to Takamori?" he asked warmly, seemingly more than just curious. We sat down cross-legged on our pillows. He began by quoting the sentence by Father William Johnston I had cited in my note: "I believe that God is the mystery of mysteries and that when we meet God, we can only say that we experience Nothing or Emptiness."

"Do you agree?" he asked.

I was ready for him. I pulled out a page of Johnston quotations from my Nepalese shoulder bag I had bought, years back, in Hong Kong. I offered another Johnston insight: "We used to say that dialogue between the religions is necessary for world peace. Now we can say that dialogue between the religions is necessary for world survival."

"I don't understand that first citation in my letter to you," I explained. "Though I'd like to, especially since," I bragged, "I just completed a Christian-Zen charismatic retreat with Father Johnston, and trust you can interpret the quote for me."

"Actually," I went on, after a silent, nervous pause in which he said nothing, "I certainly agree with most everything Father Johnston says, even if I don't always understand. But I sure do want to ask you what you think about dialogue between religions." Father Oshida winced, a look of kind disdain on his face. "Too many questions," he declared. "Intellectual, not spiritual." I felt chagrinned and completely undone since I had prepared for this exact moment so carefully. And now, too many questions, when I had hardly begun my questions.

He inquired instead about my wife and children, our family life in Taiwan, and my being a professor. He asked nothing about my faith, my Catholicism, my Christian-Zen experience. Then he got up, sat behind his desk, and politely waved goodbye.

Daily morning Eucharist at the Omido chapel the week that I stayed at Takamori was like nothing I had experienced before. I entered the chapel darkness and silence with a deep bow, my palms placed together in the traditional Buddhist *gassho* style. Father Oshida sat utterly still, a single candle on an upright log next to him. For a vestment, he wrapped himself in a beige-white garment that covered his head and hands. Usually, a dozen or so staff and Japanese and foreign guests sat cross-legged on cushions meditating, with one or two on their knees or sitting on a simple stool.

Father always wished to have the altar prepared just so, with a deep reverence for "the *logos* of a table." Thomas Merton would have referred to it as the "mystical table.[12] The *logos* of this mystical table was a wooden board on the floor, three white altar linens, and a stoneware pottery chalice centered in place. For the ritual of washing hands, there was a bowl of pure Koizumi spring water with white gravel gleaming in the bottom. Beside the altar was a large, venerable-looking clay pot sitting on a block of wood.

I sensed Father Oshida's enormous respect for tradition, the dignity of the moment, for what was taking place before our eyes, within and for each person. Everyone seemed completely present and aware of the miracle unfolding before us. As for Father Oshida, he was for me, in Merton's terms, "one whose mind and heart are integrated and illuminated by grace." He was the *holokleros* in Orthodox spirituality, the one St. Paul prays that we all become.[13]

We began Mass in profound silence, breathing deeply. Our silent, collective breaths imbued the entire Eucharist. One of Father Oshida's disciples, Reverend Chiemi Ishii, a female Protestant minister, has hauntingly described the unfolding of the chapel liturgy:

> As we sit in *zazen*, we become engulfed by the silence of the Omido. It penetrates our bodies, becoming clear and transparent, hypnotic, and tangible, as time passes. Chanting psalms, we breathe in and out, long and deeply, coordinating our breath together in the breath we share. "I" disappears, words are born anew, only to vanish. The breath of all beings, their groaning, and pain become a soundless Voice, coming into being and disappearing. Father Oshida says, "To pray is to ride on breath." Such a prayer is what exists here in the Omido, the prayer of Takamori Soan.[14]

The "Voice" that Chiemi Ishii cites is a key sacred word for Father Oshida. He used it repeatedly throughout his teaching, writing, and speaking engagements. It is the Hebrew reality of *Bat Kol*—the Voice of God. "The Voice" is the divine revelation through sound. It is an utterance announcing God's reactions to events, and God's voicing His will and judgments.[15]

For Oshida, it is the Voice of God.

Reverend Ishii's "coming into being and disappearing" is a mystical koan or word-puzzle. To my mind, it invokes death and resurrection. It echoes the descriptions of the disciples' experience of the risen Christ. At the breakfast BBQ, for example, where Jesus cooks fish and bread at the Sea of Tiberias for his disciples (John 21: 1-14), he is visible, in the flesh, then disappears. Christ disappears in his death upon the Cross, then appears again in a conversation with followers on the road to Emmaus and the silent meal they share which follows (Luke 24: 13-35), in an encounter with Mary Magdalene at the empty tomb (John 20: 14-18), and in the appearance to "doubting Thomas" and the disciples in the locked Upper Room, he does not linger but disappears again.

Analogously, in Father Oshida's Mass at Takamori's Omido, worshippers disappear in the silence, breath, chant, and word, then emerge to their consciousness of all Creation's silent groaning for salvation, only to lose themselves again in the silence which itself becomes the Voice of God.

After reading the Gospel, moved by Word and Spirit, Father Oshida would turn to some event or person from deep inside his consciousness.

His speech and demeanor were softly dramatic, like a Kabuki actor. One moment he could be gentle and tender then pointed and angry, or then sounding an ecstatic chortle. He spoke in Japanese, then in English, and sometimes in French, depending on the guests. He would intone Latin hymns to the Blessed Virgin Mary. His preaching evoked tears and amusement, while his topics always proved diverse. He weaved together disparate thoughts. On one morning after his homily, at the Prayer of the Faithful, he might pray for the disabled, the captured and jailed, and martyrs outside the visible church. The next morning his prayer might be local and immediate, giving thanks for the mystical gifts shared with the community by a visiting female Japanese monk. He might note the loving self-giving of a Takamori groundskeeper or the daily threat facing neighboring peasant rice farmers from polluters and developers. "Forgiveness is unity," he would declare.

At the beginning of the Offertory, Father Oshida did something utterly new to me in the Mass. He lit a fire made from twigs and paper set in the clay pot beside the altar, returned to his cushion, and began to sing softly. As the flames crackled, the smoke rose through an opening in the chapel's peak. The ashes settled in our room.

After the consecration, Father Oshida asked that this Body and Blood give us courage and simplicity. "Let God take us in his strength to the abyss," he prayed. The snapping of fire, the snowfall of ashes, and the faint fragrance of smoke and incense joined in a shared moment of sacred presence as we handed Christ's Body and Blood from person to person. For a brief period, the Mass was a mystical transformation. We breathed in the cup and plate, the chant, the tabernacle and altar, even Father Oshida's vestments and downcast eyes, outside of time, beyond self, seemed consumed in the body and blood and the fire.

My tentative, hesitant, Catholic self became unmoored. In the rising flames and falling ashes, I was discovering my more true self that was riding the breath of all being, coming into being and disappearing in the soundless Voice, suspended in the prayer of Takamori.

The significance of fire in the Mass should have been clear to me but was not. Father Oshida had a deep reverence for sacred spaces and holy places all over the world, notably the ancient cultures of Japan, and most especially that of the Ainu aborigines (Aynu) also known as the Ezo (蝦夷) in Japanese historical texts, an Asian ethnic group native to Japan and Siberia. Quite possibly, the opening in the chapel ceiling originated in the Ainu custom of ventilating indoor fires for warmth and cooking.[16]

In *Confession of a Fisherman (Ryooshi no Kokuhaku)*, Father Oshida's Japanese translation of the Gospel of John, he asks:

Omido altar setting for Mass on the chapel floor

> Why does fire attract us? When wood goes through transformation and becomes fire, we feel some sure presence behind the flame that may burn out soon. That sure presence . . . comes to us with certainty. On this fire we cook and we eat and exchange our presence. It was in that friendship circle and gathering ("madoi," まどい "enkyo" 円居)[17] that human beings started burning offerings to God and offered their food cooked on the fire. The sense of that sure presence that people felt through history was shared by the fishermen at the sea of Galilee. That sure presence is with us now being all the substance of the material world that surrounds us.[18]

It was not until years later that I remembered the connection between God and fire in the Hebrew Bible when Moses hears God speak: "Out of the heavens he let you hear his voice . . . out of the earth, he let you see his great fire, and you heard him speaking out of the fire" (Deuteronomy 4: 33).

In the New Testament, John the Baptist, referring to Jesus, says: "I am baptizing you with water, for repentance, but the one who is coming after me is mightier than I. I am not worthy to carry his sandals. He will baptize you with the Holy Spirit and fire" (Matt. 3: 11). The "sure presence" of fire at Oshida's Eucharist reminded me of my baptism. Let Fire be a portion of the liturgy of every Mass, I thought. Its presence would announce the Holy Spirit transforming the bread and wine into the Body and Blood of Jesus, our Christ. It would herald a continuing Pentecost when in the form of "tongues as of fire," the Spirit rested on the heads of the disciples (Acts 2: 2).

Everyone participated in daily chores at Takamori Soan. My job during my first visit was working in the strawberry bed, cultivating and transplanting. Of course, everything had to be done correctly and contemplatively, in Father Oshida's "way." We were to learn through experience, by trial and error, but most importantly, by observing and listening in silence.

One day several of us went to the Takamori rice paddy to harvest the late August rice. After everyone had a good laugh enjoying how there were no rubber boots big enough in Japan to fit my size 14 feet, we grabbed scythes and set to work. I thought I was doing a pretty good job cutting the rice stalks close to the ground and stacking them in tepee-like cones, although my tepees kept collapsing.

"No, no, never *that* way," Oshida shouted at me, "but *this* way."

He demonstrated "*this* way," by cutting and stacking gracefully and precisely. I grasped the beautiful difference in the way he held the rice stalks and cut, placing them in elegant stacks standing in a perfect row. I simply couldn't get it right.

"Listen to the rice," Oshida urged me. "Be the farmer. The farmer listens. The rice tells him when it wants to be planted, fertilized, weeded, and harvested. The rice knows how it should be cut and stacked. The rice doesn't read it out of a book. Listen, listen, listen. The rice will tell you everything."

After a while, I stood back and watched the beautiful scene of the harvest unfolding all around me, experiencing Reverend Ishii's words describing the laborious yet delicate work of rice farming at 3,300 feet elevation. "There is nothing comparable to the beauty of people working in the same rice field with Father Oshida saying, "'The work must sink deeply into one's body,'" she writes. "We are also cultivated in this effort . . . because our wrongs and distress fall into nature. Takamori's rice fields have the power to absorb them."[19]

When I returned home from Japan and told Father Mark Delery at St. Joseph's Abbey of my stunning introduction to Father Oshida's spirituality, he suggested he be invited to Mary House to give a "Christian-Zen" retreat. My wife Bonnie and I sponsored his visit with the help of a lay group we had founded called the New Covenant Community. In the late 1970s and early 1980s, Father Oshida gave "contemplative retreats" focusing on Christ in a formally Japanese Zen Buddhist style at Mary House and Holy Cross Abbey in Berryville, Virginia. He eschewed the term "Christian-Zen."

The Holy Innocents
and the Kodomo in the Womb
Takamori, Japan September Conference

One early summer day at my home in Massachusetts, I received a mysterious invitation from Father Oshida to attend a week-long meeting to be held on September 23-30, 1981, at Takamori Soan, his community center in the Japanese Alps. The invitation was completely unexpected. His letter referred to a "September Meeting." Behind this innocuous title, Father Oshida was gathering peacemakers at an extreme moment of world change. He was inviting people engaged with the sufferings of humanity and the afflicted, who lived among the poor, served them, and were poor themselves. I felt honored to attend.

At the Conference, Father Oshida welcomed us by saying that "Both the afflicted and those who sit side by side with them as recipients of the gift of redemptive suffering for others, are bearers of the Cross on their way to the Father. Let us go on a pilgrimage together." His words were serious while his face was smiling.

Then he clarified why we were gathering at the Takamori hermitage to meditate together. He felt we were experiencing a *kairos* moment, a time of crisis for the world.

> The desert of materialistic civilization is expanding exponentially, and I am deeply alarmed by the rampant development of nuclear weapons around the world, and the lack of moral stamina to control them. Nature is being destroyed, and there is spiritual ruin accompanying this blight. Heads of state and leaders from various walks of life are groping in the dark with no clear sense of direction. I fear universal devastation throughout the earth. In the course that civilization is now taking, we feel something looming in which we anticipate the barren abyss where no one could be saved from unfathomable darkness.[20]

To an outsider who was unfamiliar with Father Oshida, his vision of the conference might seem quixotic, impractical, and overstated. But he went on to say that he was not interested in a phenomenal analysis of present real-

A still quiet ecstasy
Photo Source Unknown

ity. He wanted us to hear a call to listen to "the Voice concealed in history" (*bat kol*).

"Jesus asked for this assembly," he explained. "This is Bethlehem." He recalled the scripture, "Foxes have dens and birds of the sky have nests, but the Son of Man has nowhere to rest his head" (Luke 9: 58).

> We have been asked to come to a place where there is no pillow. It is the way to the Father, the Cross. I was longing for a new horizon and perceived the time ripe for capable persons who shared others' pain and suffering and were living a spiritual life to undertake a different historical orientation. I invite you to leave yourselves behind on this pilgrimage, to disappear and obey the Voice of God. It is a duty of conscience.

To me, Father Oshida's viewpoint regarding this crisis moment in world history was prescient and prophetic. Has his perspective not been realized in the present 21st Century of the Covid-19 virus pandemic, the long legacy of environmental degradation, the steadily rising threat of nuclear annihilation, and the end of the world as we have known it?

I was mystified that Father Oshida had invited me to the Conference. I was not a peacemaker or spiritual leader who lived among and served the poor. Then I recalled a *sesshin* with Father Oshida that I had attended at Mary House in Spencer, Massachusetts.

At the early morning Eucharist, the Presider, Father Jim Campbell OP, a member of Father Oshida's Dominican order, had come from South Carolina to join the *sesshin*. He introduced himself briefly. When he mentioned somewhat sheepishly that he had been an American Air Force bomber pilot during World War II, and had dropped bombs over Japan, Father Oshida suddenly roared with laughter. "Aha!" he cackled. "I was in the Japanese Anti-Aircraft Corp. I was shooting at you while you were bombing me!"

The two war veterans hooted and howled, enjoying this unexpected encounter, or you might say, re-encounter. The *sesshin* dissolved into laughter, with all of us lapping up this moment of inexplicable joy, which only former enemies could know as they danced about hugging one another in forgiveness and gratitude.

It happened to be the Feast of Mary's Assumption into heaven, August 15, and Father Oshida had asked Jim to read the Gospel and give the homily at our morning Mass. The Gospel describes newly pregnant Mary's visit to see her relative, Elizabeth, who is in her sixth month of pregnancy.

> Mary set out and traveled to the hill country in haste to a town of Judah, where she entered the house of Zechariah and greeted Elizabeth. When Elizabeth heard Mary's greeting, the infant leaped in her womb, and Elizabeth, filled with the Holy Spirit, cried out in a loud voice and said, "Blessed are you among women, and blessed is the fruit of your womb. And how does this happen to me, that the mother of my Lord should come to me? For at the moment the sound of your greeting reached my ears, the infant in my womb leaped for joy. Blessed are you who believed that what was spoken to you by the Lord would be fulfilled" Luke (1: 39-45).

After reading the passage, Jim said that instead of giving a homily, he would like each of us to act out physically our response to the Gospel. We all sat there shyly, no one making a move, especially the men. How on earth bring off an embodied actualization of being pregnant?

Quietly Father Oshida got up from his cushion, wrapped himself in his prayer shawl, and lay down on the floor curled in a fetal position— a baby in the womb, a Holy Innocent? We were all mystified, wondering what he was doing. I was dumbfounded. He lay there in silence for some time as if he were sleeping. When he sat up, he began murmuring in a low voice, seemingly waking up.

"Thank you, Father Campbell," he said. "You made me experience the mystery of the pulsation of blood: the 'things of heaven' (Col. 3: 2). Jesus was aware in the womb of pulsation. He did not become Jesus only when he gained consciousness. You made me feel the will of God, the original sign of the Cross, the flowing of water and blood."

I speculated that Father Oshida had only invited me to this Conference because the Unborn had touched his spirit, that he felt the child in the womb to be close to the heart of the conference. He had regularly received the newsletter I originated and edited, "Reflections—a Healing Dialogue for Women and Men Who Experience Abortion." He knew I was involved for many years with persons who had faced abortion. So, I assumed that's why I was there.

When it came time for me to speak, Father Oshida introduced me. "Lucien Miller is a professor at the University of Massachusetts. He is engaged in salvation work through listening to the voices of women who, because of their conscious hearts, cry for painful respect despite having committed the sin of abortion."

I was speechless as I heard his word "sin." I felt its sting. I knew the story of abortion in America and the broadness of its practice in Japan. I knew the grief that so often accompanies it. I did not want to say anything that would add to the pain of Japanese participants. But what held me spellbound by his word "sin" was our collective sin as Americans. Who can forget the Vietnam War, indelibly imprinted in our minds in the picture of the "Napalm Girl," the little naked nine-year-old Kim Phuc Phan Thi, running toward the viewer, her back on fire with American napalm from an air attack during the Vietnam War?[21]

Synh Cong "Nick" Ut Photo
Associated Press

That photo came to mind as Father Oshida spoke of abortion. What is more, the Japanese woman sitting next to me at the Conference had introduced herself by saying she was a *hibakusha* (被爆者), a "blasted one," the Japanese word for a survivor of the second A-Bomb dropped on Nagasaki. The bomb's epicenter was fifteen hundred feet from the Catholic Cathedral of the Immaculate Conception—incinerating the priests and parishioners inside— her home town and place of worship. She was to be the next speaker.

Nagasaki A-Bomb
August 9, 1945

I stood up, intending to speak, but because of Father Oshida's word "sin,"
my bad conscience over our Vietnam War, and my co-speaker being a victim of our second atomic bomb, I could not find words. I sat down. I wanted
to weep but was unable.

"We Americans did terrible things to you Japanese in the war," I whispered to my Japanese partner. She arose and bowed to me. It seemed a gesture of sorrow and total empathy. "We did terrible things too," she said, sigh-
ing deeply. "You have seen the Memorial Wood here at Takamori." I nodded
in response. She then encouraged me to speak. "Please go on, Mille-san." I
did get up, and I went on.

"*Domo arigato gozaimasu*," I said to my companion, returning her bow.
"Thank you so very much." "Help me, Jesus," I murmured to myself, under
my breath.

"Dear Friends," I said. "How grateful I am to be here among you. And
how unworthy I am. I do not serve the poor of the world, nor live among
them, nor am I poor myself, as so many of you. The word "sin" pains me so

much—I cannot speak of the sin of abortion nor of women's sins when I am so conscious of my own as an American.

"I would like to share what happened after I arrived at Takamori for our conference. Mr. Toshio Kanamitsu from the Japanese National Broadcasting Company (NHK) took me aside, and tenderly laid before me a volume of words and illustrations he had helped edit, entitled *Unforgettable Fire.*[22] He quietly opened the book to its introduction, noted a bookmark where the illustrations and their captions began, then, without another word, he left me to meditate alone on what I saw before me. The brief introduction noted that some thirty years after the Second World War, the NHK invited the *Hibakusha,* who had survived the first American A-Bomb at Hiroshima, August 6, 1945, to submit a drawing or painting together with a sentence or paragraph to describe their experience. These respondents were not artists nor writers, but who were simply present there when 'Little Boy,' the American codename for the Hiroshima atomic bomb, fell from the skies."

I examined one painting and read aloud its caption:

> "I was suddenly frightened by a terrible sight 40 to 50 meters from Shukkeien Garden. There was a charred body of a woman standing frozen in a running posture with one leg lifted and her baby tightly clutched in her arms. Who on earth could she be?" Yasuo Yamagata, aged 49.

"As I try to speak to you, the photo of the Vietnamese girl on whom we Americans dropped napalm, and the memories and portraits of Japanese survivors in *Unforgettable Fire* invade my mind.

"I'm so sorry," I said. "I personally apologize to you, Japanese friends, for what we Americans did to you with our A-bombs. And yet, how grateful I am to be here, to learn from all of you of your work and your lives among the planet's poor and on our poor planet.

"What I have to share is 'small potatoes,'" I remarked, "as we say in the States, compared to what you all have talked about and experienced in serving the poor, living among them, and being poor yourselves. But blame it on Father Oshida! He's the one who invited me." Everyone smiled ingratiatingly. Some laughed out loud as I pointed my finger at Father Oshida. But they looked perplexed too. What were my "small potatoes" all about?

"In his invitation letter," I went on, "Father Oshida asked us 'to listen to the Voice,' to turn to our experience of the Absolute, the Unborn Sphere, and examine our hearts concerning those who suffer and our vocations to empathetic suffering. My particular service has been with women who experience abortion, and with the husbands or lovers, families and loved ones, and doctors and nurses who share that experience. I am here today because I have been involved over the last ten years with the issue of abortion in the United States, encouraging a healing dialogue among those who experience abortion. As I am listening now to the Voice, I hear the voices of the unwillingly destroyed Unborn from the womb. I am sharing the tears of those who are currently involved in the destruction of human life who may also be unconsciously asking for compassion and understanding.

"Over the last few days, we have shared a great deal about what we call in English a 'holocaust,' massive losses of innocent human life. We've been talking about a potential holocaust when nuclear bombs would destroy massive numbers of us. We have remembered the momentous holocausts of the middle decades of the 20th century. These tragedies include the destruction of Jews and other "undesirables" in Germany, our American A-Bombs dropped on the innocent in Hiroshima and Nagasaki, our fire-bombing of Tokyo and Dresden, and, just a decade ago, our saturation bombings of Vietnam and Cambodia.

"The issue for me at the center of our Conference is the child, *kodomo*—the innocent victim of a present holocaust—the sacrifice of human life in America and around the world through abortion. These are 'small potatoes,' the wee ones, the *kodomo*."

Some in the audience looked disturbed, as though they had scar tissue like my college students back home when I mentioned God or sin. Noticing this, I remarked, "I feel sensitive talking to you about this because there are many abortions in Japan as in America, and your feelings might be hurt. Perhaps you have experienced abortion, or known it in your own families."

At this moment, I lost my bearings and sat down again. I had evoked pain. The room was silent.

After a long pause, the woman speaker who had survived the Nagasaki American A-Bomb tugged at my sleeve with one hand. She raised her free hand, palm lifting upward, gently urging me to go on. I nodded gratefully, took a deep breath, and stood up again.

" We need to consider abortion, my friends," I continued, "because many times when we are talking about ecology or war, it is easy to identify who or what is the enemy, the 'other.' But in the case of abortion, we are touching on something and someone that affects the lives of each one of us here, *kodomo*, the unborn who are not 'other' but are ourselves. The unwanted and aborted remind me very much of what you were talking about earlier—the unwelcome minority in Japan, the *burakumin* (*fuyōna shōsū-ha* 不要な少数派), or the Untouchable in India. There is something so human and so inhumane, no matter in what country it is, about rejecting the weakest, the unacceptable, the person who is in some way inconvenient, and I think of the Unborn who is unwanted as being parallel to the Untouchable."

After a long pause, I carried on.

"I see a kind of spider's web where all these different concerns and these distinct areas of suffering we have discussed are intimately related. In my Catholic faith and many of your beliefs and cultures, we consider the womb a sacred place, and we hold sacred the relationship between mother and child. The womb is the place of destiny. Among the Jewish prophets, it is a place of divine calling. 'Can a mother forget a child at her breast, or can a mother forget the child in her womb?' one of them asks. 'But' says Yahweh, 'even should she forget, I will never forget you'" (Isaiah 49: 15).

"Isn't it true," I asked, "that all of you in one way or another are honoring this intimate holy alliance in the work you do among the poor, the relation you have with the unwanted, the untouchable, or the unborn? Let us be aware of this holy alliance this week and for the rest of our lives. Let us never forget."

Several bowed, their heads in their hands. I thought it best to end my talk, not knowing what else to do.

"One last thing I'd like to share," I said. "Call it 'baby-talk,' the vulgar American metaphorical language linking the child with the atomic bomb. Thomas Merton wrote ironically about the making of the Hiroshima atomic bomb in the United States. Did you read his article we passed around? The workmen who made the bomb used the codeword 'Little Boy.' I do not know the impact of a Japanese translation, but the English 'Little Boy' is a terrible ugly joke. The code phrase, 'babies, satisfactorily born,' designated the moment the bombs had been successfully detonated.

"The name for 'atom bomb' in Chinese, is *yuanzi dan* 原子彈, in Thomas

Merton's literal rendering, 'Original Child.' Merton goes on to discern something ugly and ironic but also very evil in these associations between the bomb and the child. Mr. Wada in his talk, and a paper I read by him in English, talked about hope for the future, he used the phrase in Japanese *haha no jida*i (母の時代), 'The age of the mother.' I spoke with him a little bit later. He noted to me the qualities that make a mother a mother, and how these qualities hold hope for our future. I thought hard about this: if the mother-child relationship aborts in the womb, the future might be bleak.

"However, I am hopeful. I do feel that the more people understand, the more we reflect together, the more possibility there is of hope. Let us focus on the vulnerable child in the womb. Let us be compassionate with those who destroy them or save them. Let us be in solidarity with one another, and all who dedicate themselves to saving lives, born or unborn. They are one with us today. We are one with them. Thank you."

Last Days

Father Oshida Death-Mask

Father Oshida died a few years after he participated in the International Interfaith Pilgrimage for Peace and Life (1994-1995). It was an extraordinary walk from Auschwitz to Hiroshima, marking the 50th anniversary of the end of World War II. A journey of 10,000 miles through some eighteen countries scarred by old conflicts and the wounds of present-day wars. It was an act of collective remembering, reparation, compassion, and healing meant for the transformation of self and world.

He struggled all his life with tuberculosis (he called TB his "Zen Master"). He must have known that the long peace journey would be too much for his physical condition. Following the pilgrimage, his health steadily declined. Father Shigeto Vincent-Marie Oshida O.P. "returned to heaven" while residing at Takamori, November 6, 2003. He was 81.[23]

When Father Oshida died, this letter was sent from Takamori Soan, written by Sister Maria Kawasumi, a devoted member of the Takamori Soan community, dated December 22, 2003.

Peace in God.

As many of you may already know, Father Oshida went Home on the eve of November 6th, concluding his 8 years struggling against cardiac failure. Having been in and out of hospital and unable to come back to live at Takamori Soan with its rigorous climate, he finally spent his last three months at Takamori, enjoying the natural beauty of autumn in the mountains. Although there were times when he had to bear pain beyond description, he departed peacefully, passing over to the other shore in his last deep sleep. Everything being washed away, his expression was so beautiful that it impressed everyone who came to his side.

"All abandoning to God . . . God is wonderful . . ." he started murmuring two days before his death, looking at the falling leaves from his room. Then his murmur turned into a chant. "God is wonderful. God is wonderful, God is wonderful. Amen. Amen. Amen. Amen!"

They were the last words he uttered from the depth of his being.

In the years ahead, following my Charismatic-Zen retreat with Father Johnston in Taiwan and the visit to Takamori in 1976, and attendance there at the September Conference in 1981, my pilgrimage compass in the 1990s decade was pointing East and Southeast to India, China, and Sri Lanka. My sense of the other side of the mountain would culminate in these countries through serendipitous experiences of the poor. Again I was guided by Thomas Merton toward the pure of heart and the wounded presence of Holy Innocents. My mysterious reorientations would always happen by chance, coincidental by-products of deliberate academic pursuits.

India

In 1990-1991 I had a year-long sabbatical the second half of which my wife Bonnie and I were to spend in China collecting ethnic minority folktales. We had no idea what to do in the first half. Should we stay home while I was on leave from teaching the Spring semester 1990? Should Bonnie continue working as a therapist while I conducted my research? I had attended a two-year weekend Faculty Seminar at Columbia University on Asian Literatures in the late-1980s. I fell in love with India and Indian classical literature, most notably the *Bhagavad-Gita* ("The Song of God"). The late Indologist, Barbara Miller, one of its most distinguished English interpreters and translators, had exquisitely taught the course. Bonnie and I began to ask ourselves about India as a possibility. I could study folk literature that traveled back and forth along the ancient Southern Silk Road connecting India, Burma, and Yunnan, China, and we would explore India together. I had no background in Indian studies but took a chance and applied for and received a grant for my project from the American Institute for Indian Studies.

I asked Dr. Miller where we should go in all of India. "Mysore" (Mysuru), she answered immediately. Her answer proved prophetic for there in Karnataka, South India we found a dream come true. A Brigittine Sisters' convent ran a hostel for travelers. The Sisters lived in a garden paradise of giant palms, flowers, and birds. They offered rooms for rent to travelers like us to sustain their lives of religious enclosure. After living in the convent, the citizens of a near-by village of poor Indian families befriended us and treated us like favorite deities. And this happened because one of my graduate students was from Mysore, and she insisted that we contact the Bishop of Mysore for a place to stay, and it was he who located us with the Brigittines. Being directed to Mysore and the Bishop had to have led us to this beautiful abode. Was it just luck, or an act of divine providence?

The Year of the Girl-Child

I experienced poor Indian girls and boys as innocents, sacred beings that my wife and I encountered during our sabbatical leave on the streets and byways of Mysore, Bangalore, and Calcutta (Bengaluru, Kolkata) in Southern India. These children, along with the sick and dying elders, were Holy Innocents to me because they had done nothing wrong, except to be subject to India's dreadful caste system. They were born in the wrong caste in the wrong place at the wrong time. In 1990, the year of our first sabbatical in India, my sensitivity to female children was amplified because 1990-1991 was the United Nations designated "Year of the Girl-Child" in India.

Four "Girl-Childs" moved me immensely in Mysore, Bangalore, and Calcutta. (For all I know, they were *Nakusas* or *Naroshis*—words for unwanted nameless girls in India, the hidden suffering). I gave them my Hindi names for them, sensing who I felt they were.

Aabha—She Who Glows

Aabha was a little girl of perhaps five or six years old who worked in the coal yard around the railroad tracks, a few blocks from our residence in Mysore. I used to see her when I was riding my bicycle on my way to the Manasagangotri Research Institute. Gliding through the Untouchables section of Mysore, I would see her tiny lone figure darting in and out among the dust bins and piles of coal. She was filthy dirty, covered with coal dust, her clothes a cloud of gray, as she carried pieces of coal hither and yon, somehow going about her duties, whatever they were. And yet, for me, she gleamed. Her face, black with railroad grime, shone brightly, as though from some interior light, her fearless eyes full of life, play, and undaunted vim.

Piki-Cuckoo

I nicknamed this tiny girl Piki, "cuckoo" because she was furtive yet brave, and had a distinctive cuckoo-like voice. I would always see her upon landing at the Bangalore airport when I exited with my baggage. She wore a see-through sleeveless pinafore and no underwear. I guessed she was six and that she was not raised by her parents, whom I thought of as cuckoos who plagiarize and lay their eggs in another bird's nest for rearing their babies. In India, cuckoos are sacred to Kamadeva, the god of desire and longing. Piki became holy to me and full of desire to help. She would charge up to me ahead of the other urchins seeking work and call out "Cooey?" or "Coucou?" (meaning "want help?" in French). She learned these words as "Hi there!" from disembarking French tourists. The sound of her call was like a soft knock or the gentle afternoon murmuring of a mourning dove. She was so small that I might have held her in the palm of my hand. Standing up, she was a little taller than my bag. So try as she might, she could not carry it. Relinquishing the effort of squeezing the handle, she would pat-pat the sides of the suitcase as I made my way to the taxi as if to assist me in getting aboard.

Darshini—the One Who Blesses

Once during a rainstorm in Calcutta, the taxi I was riding in pulled up at a traffic stop. Immediately a teenage girl with dark intoxicating eyes appeared at my window, holding a baby in her arms. She was begging despite the storm, and she placed her hand firmly against my window. I did not perceive her hand as a beggar's. She was, for me, an ascetic or *sadhu* asking for alms, practicing *bhiksha*, on her way to salvation and transcendence. She would have laughed had I told her how I saw her. In her eyes, I found my different story of her, as if she were a bearer of blessings for me, an incarnation presenting to me from another life. I wanted to think of her as reincarnated from a more blessed state than her present life of struggle in the deep currents of the River Poverty.

Before the traffic light turned green, she was off sprinting barefoot through the rain, like an Olympic champion, clinging to her baby as she became lost in the darkness of her ghetto. Shame struck me in retrospect when I realized that I had not given her a rupee, not a dime. I shall never forget that haunting vision of the rain-soaked madonna.

Parveeni—The Star

Parveeni—The Star
Author Photo

We were driving through the Deccan plateau on our way to visit a dam on the Cauvery (Kaveria) river with our host, Father Joseph, a Catholic priest, and his two nieces, both grown-up young women. The land was dry, uninhabited desert. Along the road, we encountered a party of *shudras* breaking up stones with mallets (their life-long fate in all probability). We passed a company of bird-catchers bearing traps and paraphernalia to support their style of meager living. Finally, we came upon a home-made circus troop making camp for the night. The circus master wanted to entertain us and brought out a beautiful young girl, Parveeni, who was an acrobat and performer. The circus master set up a series of rings, and placed them standing up on one end in a descending range of diameters, at the narrow terminus of which was attached a long, cramped barrel, open at both ends, but tapering yet smaller at its tip.

Parveeni paused, breathed deeply and bowed, and wiggled her way through the narrowing hoops. She then thrust her head into the barrel opening that barely fit her. She squeezed her arms to her side and kept pushing her body into the barrel until she finally disappeared. We could hear her struggling inside, kicking and moaning. Tension transfixed all our faces. After five or ten minutes, she emerged, very much disheveled, her shoulders, knees, and toes red and raw. She bowed to us visitors who had witnessed her feat, then took her place among the other performers. The circus master smiled gleefully, assuming we were pleased.

Father Joseph's two nieces were sobbing, weeping for the gypsy girl, her torture, and her slavery. She had no other future. "What did he say?" I asked the nieces. "He said," one of them remarked, shuddering, "This is what we think of girls in India."

We complained about this exhibition of torture of a Girl-Child to Father Joseph. He dressed down the circus master who seemed chagrined and humiliated. "She is your child," Father Joseph said. "You cannot kill her." He apologized to us onlookers and promised Father Joseph that Parveeni never again would star in that acrobatic trick. He smiled at us in the end, but would he keep his promise? We shall never know.

What was it about these four Girl-Childs that struck me so forcefully that I want to celebrate them in writing? Each raised questions I could not answer. Each was a koan I could not solve. I did not know them—their contexts, names, ages, familial links, or native dialects.

What could I do for them? The answer was a phrase that came to me while I was holding what proved to be my last vigil at an abortion clinic, "Be there." In other words, instead of protesting abortion, an inner, divine voice of conscience told me to just "be" with the women and men who were experiencing this quiet murder of an innocent. I created a newsletter called "Reflections" to promote a healing dialogue. Through interviews and letters, I simply listened without judging them. These simple acts proved compassionate and reparative for them and me as well. My vigils had added to their pain and mine. Listening opened locked doors.

Had I thought of the phrase "Be there" when encountering the Girl-Childs, I would not have known what it meant or was calling me to. While the girls' youth and winsome beauty-in-poverty had moved me, I also sensed the Japanese *wabi* that touched their presences, a rustic, solitary, and melancholy refinement. But my identification with them was not merely a matter of aesthetics. I wanted to roll up my sleeves, or at least donate to the Brigittine Guest House, where we stayed. Our money would buy food, clothing, and medical care. But nothing I experienced about them or wanted practically to do for them explained the mysterious motive to "draw near" and "just be" with them. My future encounter with a leper would reinvigorate for me the meaning of this mysterious invitation I felt to engage the lived-reality of the Girl-Child poverty.

Fadi, The Market Leper

My encounter with a leper in 1990 in a marketplace garden of flowers was a powerful epiphany for me. It was an awakening similar to Merton's awakening at Polonnaruwa before the Buddhist sculptures that had "jerked him clean out" of his ordinary perceptions.

Soon after Bonnie and I had taken up residence at our hostel with the Brigittine Sisters, we went on our first of many bike-rides to the Saturday Mysore open market. We spied with enchantment the redolent rows of fresh flowers, fragrant conical piles of pungent spices, radiant baskets of fruit, and everywhere, hanging rows of marigold, jasmine, and tuberose leis. The clothes that adorned the people in the market, as they milled about, buying and selling flowers, captivated our attention. The women were adorned in vivid, patterned, multi-colored saris that draped over their shoulders. Some were dressed in loose trousers and long body-length tunics. The men wore *dhoti* pajamas and long blouses that fell to their waist or knees. The Sikhs among them donned traditional turbans.

Just after we had bought ourselves two wrist bracelets of fragrant jasmine, I turned about, ready to walk away. I looked behind me and there, sitting cross-legged in a tiny garden between two rows of sweet-scented potted gardenias was a leper wearing a *dhoti*, his single swatch of white cloth wrapped around his loins. His all-but-naked sweating black body seemed to shine in the morning sunlight.

Immediately, I felt his piercing dark eyes riveted on mine. I returned his gaze and sat down before him, crossing my legs. I bowed in greeting, my hands raised, joined at the palms in prayer. He lowered his body to me in welcome and affirmation. His black eyes were sunk deep in his dark face swathed in wrinkles of sorrow and the lesions of leprosy—finger stubs, missing toes, mangled ears, and nose. I believed he was middle-aged, but he looked old.

I felt as if he knew something about our mutuality that I did not know. Perched squarely atop a tattered white rag he had rolled up beneath him, he had the wounded look of Jesus on the Cross and possessed an inner calm like a sitting Buddha. Soon we sat in silence, our eyes turned to the ground between us, sharing a mutual presence.

For several weeks after, on Saturday mornings, I would return to the marketplace with Bonnie to see "Fadi," my Hindi nickname for my leper-friend, meaning "Redeemer," for such he was or seemed to be. Within me, I experienced his suffering as being redemptive. Every visit, I would find him at his same sacred spot in his scented garden. Despite his suffering the blight of disfigurement to face and hands and social isolation, he invariably smiled a broad welcoming smile when I came up to him.

"We are brothers," he intimated silently. "Brothers!" It was true—but I did not know the half of it.

On my last visit with him, I had a moment of spiritual seeing and discernment in this interaction between my deepest being and my guru-leper. We were face-to-face, mirroring one another and looking deeply into the other's eyes, and this moment changed me forever.[24] Suddenly, I sensed my link to him in a causal sense. I was somehow responsible for his suffering. His leprosy was, in a way, an unknown part and parcel of my being and my sinfulness. His disease was redemptive, not only for him but for me as well, if not for the world. My realization was illogical, but in the depth of my being, I sensed it utterly a fact. I felt I was looking at him, "whom I had pierced"—Jesus.

I cannot explain this marketplace awakening any other way. What I do know is that our communion was joyful and infectious in a healthy, happy way. We had cried and laughed. We had shared spiritual joy, an inherent, inner aliveness.[25] Deep within my soul, I heard a call to serve the afflicted poor.

Saint Damien of Molokai, Redemptive Suffering

St. Damien Shortly Before His Death
Photo Source Wiki

Why had I intuited that the suffering of my Fadi was redemptive?

Hidden within me surfaced a memory of hearing about St. Damien and his outpost of lepers on Molokai Island in Hawaii. I had wanted to visit the colony when I was a student at the East-West Center at the University of Hawaii. I even tried to descend the cliff above the settlement, but it was off-limits to the public. I wished to learn about them and their lives, and possibly befriend an exile. However, a handful of lepers were milling about on the top of the precipice. We chatted for a while, and I learned that Father Damien, their founding father, had himself died of leprosy while taking care of his people. They were a gentle group, for the most part, friendly. I remember being surprised that their disfigurement did not repulse me. So this is leprosy I said to myself—facial wounds, one person with missing lips, another whose twisted ears were scarcely visible, others stumped feet, contorted noses or missing fingers.

Saint Marianne Cope attended Father Damien when he died of leprosy in his leper colony in Molokai, and she carried on his work after his death in 1889. She once remarked of lepers, "Make life as pleasant as possible for our fellow creatures whom God has chosen to afflict."[26] I found her insight almost unbearable. Was leprosy God's choice for them?

Mother Teresa certainly thought so, the role not only of lepers but the poorest of the poor, the oppressed and marginalized. In them, she saw the face of Jesus. Indeed, for her, they *were* Jesus. Not only that: in their co-redemptive suffering, they were joined to Jesus's Passion and death—not as punishment for "God does not punish," she insisted, but to atone with Jesus for the sins of the world, including my own.[27]

> She insisted that lepers understood. In a talk to a group of "our lepers," as she called them, she drew this affirmative response:
>
> I was talking to our lepers and telling them that leprosy is a gift from God, that God can trust them so much that he gives them this terrible suffering.
>
> "Repeat that," one of them said, shaking the sleeve of her sari, "repeat that this is God's love. Those who are suffering understand you when you talk like this, Mother Teresa."[28]

And yet I have always found this leper's realization insufferable. Could I embrace it in my heart? Was this "God's love"? Again, had God chosen to afflict them? Was leprosy redemptive for the leper and the world and me?

"We are brothers," my leper friend Fadi had said. Brothers in Affliction.

Naming "Glory Boy"
Yunnan, China

In the spring of 1991, with Bonnie and my superb mentor, Bai translator and guide, Duan Shoutao, and then in the summer of 1992 on my own, I collected oral folktales of the Bai ethnic nationality around Erhai Lake near Dali in Yunnan Province, China. The Bai are one of the 56 ethnic minority groups China officially recognizes within its borders.[29]

Among the Bai
All Bai Photos by Author

One long, leisurely weekend in Dali, the summer of 1992, while recording Bai tales, I decided to take a break to go on a three-day hike by myself and climbed the 10,600-foot Cock's Foot Mountain (雞足山 *Jizu Shan*) on the northeast side of Erhai Lake. The name, "Cock's Foot," comes from the fact that there are three peaks that make up the mountain, which from a distance look like the three toes of a rooster gripping the summit.

To get to Cock's Foot, I thought it would be an especially fine beginning if I, who had once been a college oarsman and loved to row, could hire one of the many open boats I had spotted on the Western shore of Erhai, and row five miles across the lake to a tiny fishermen's village on the northeast side, Wase, where locals would direct me to the mountain, and I would begin my trek.

Early Friday morning I shouldered my backpack, and to the sound of the crowing of competing village roosters announcing the dawn, I made my way to the lakeshore by the light of morning breakfast fires coming to life, and walked to a Bai fishing village at the Erhai lakefront to try my luck.

Along the shallows, two Bai fishermen were setting their nets.

"Any chance I could hire one of your boats?" I asked some fishermen who were by the shore, mending nets, and nearly ready for a day out on the water. I had studied a little of the Bai language, but hardly enough to carry on a conversation, so we spoke in Chinese—some Bai are bilingual. One weathered fisherman was much bemused. He ogled me up and down, then with a grin, fiddled with his fishing line, pretending he did not understand me.

I repeated my request.

"You can't go out on the lake alone," an old man interjected who was standing on the shoreline. "The cadre would not allow that." He was referring to a Communist government authority, and some local rule restricting foreigners and where they could travel in Dali.

"Do you know how to row?" laughed a young boy, gawking at me, not expecting a foreigner could do anything but be guided by a Bai.

"I'm an expert," I rejoined. "I rowed for four years in college." I swept my hand over the deep blue-green lake glimmering in the morning sun, and bragged: "I could take a bunch of you Bai brothers for a rowing excursion all over Erhai!"

Heads bobbled up and down the beach, as rows of fishermen, working on their boats, howled with laughter, their mouths hanging open.

"Ha-Ha!" they bellowed in chorus. One spat. "Foreign-devil Mr. Big Pants thinks he can take us Bai on a tourist trip of Bailand."

"Bah!" joined in another. "Stinky-stale flatbread!"

He was referring to a locally famous snack, Dali Baba (大理粑粑), a barbecued flatbread stuffed with minced pork and sweet red bean paste, gone sour. No-nothing foreigners called it "pizza."

Apparently a stately white-haired gentleman wearing a white flat cap with a slight bill was impressed by my chutzpah. He was leaning against the side of a long skiff next to him.

"This is my boat," he nodded, proudly, pointing with his chin. "You can ride with us. We're headed for Wase Village on the other side of the lake."

"How perfect for me," I thought.

He paused. "She's eighteen feet long. Takes two men with double oars. No way you could ever row her by yourself, even if you were strong as a college kid."

"But," he smiled graciously, pointedly noting my middle-aged self, "you can come along for the ride."

He and his crew grabbed the boat's gunwales and dragged her over the sand, while I pushed from the rear. Once the craft was afloat, we clambered aboard, and were off.

Soon, one fisherman pulled out an erhu (二胡), a two-stringed fiddle, and started fiddling a Bai folksong with his bow. The men joined in, singing to the steady back-and-forth rhythm of the two sets of oars being pulled by two fishermen. Before long, the cloudless blue sky turned gray, and it began to rain. Back went the erhu into its carrying sack, and I pulled out of my duffle bag my rain parka. The Bai men didn't seem to mind getting wet in the least.

Someone passed around handfuls of black twisted stogies, and I—who years back used to love a good cigar—lit up too. Ugh! It tasted and smelled so foul that I nearly spat it out, but hung on, not wanting to offend my new Bai pals.

Figuring we were coasting for awhile, I saw my chance.

"Can I take a turn rowing?" I asked.

The crew started giggling, along with the smirking skipper.

"Why not?" he asked, waggishly. "Why not give my two rowing boys a rest? Hey! Grab hold of a pair of oars and take us for a tour!"

Guffaws of laughter thundered from the forecastle crew.

I stood up cautiously—the boat had started to rock in a rising breeze—and positioned my legs squarely against some staves bracing the stern rowing seat. At first I wasn't getting anywhere—men and boat were indeed heavy— and the crew let out a "we told-you-so" hoot from bow to stern.

Gradually, I angled my way along until the slight wind was at my back, and I began pulling gently, then strongly, slowly increasing the pressure.

"Look at the foreign-devil go," cried one, flabbergasted.

The disbelieving silence was palpable. Gradually, we began to pick up speed as I strained at the oars, and my new Bai friends clapped with delight.

Mr. Stinky-stale Flatbread agreed. "Wow!" he cried. "Wow!"

Someone began singing some rhythmic folksong, and everyone joined in, pounding the sides of the boat to the swing of the oars. Off we flew across Ear Lake in a cacophonous roar, heading for port at Wase Village.

When we landed, a curious fisherman father and his little son eyed us, wondering what this big strange-looking foreigner was doing tending the oars.

After we hauled the boat ashore, we tramped to their tiny hamlet, a mile or two from Wase, where they gave me directions to Cock's Foot. There were a few trails, they said, but the unmarked paths tended to go in several different directions, and disappeared off and on as you ascended. My pals had another good laugh, envisioning Big Boy hopelessly wandering the slopes of Cock's Foot.

* * * * * * *

Two-thirds of the way up the mountain, after passing through bamboo groves and scrub pines, I got lost as the trail I was following forked several times and then utterly disappeared. Luckily, I came across two Bai women, a mother and her very young daughter, who urged me to follow them. They were both wearing red vests over their white blouses, skirts, and long dark pants. The lovely girl was dressed up as though on holiday. I noticed how she had slightly embroidered her red vest at the bottom in a floral pattern, as she had her crescent-shaped headscarf covering her hair, made of multi-color circular bands of material tightly stitched together. She clung firmly with both hands to an embroidered shawl wrapped around her shoulders, within which she carefully carried a package on her back. I imagined she was traveling with something precious. I was soon to find out the nature of the treasure she was hiding in her shawl.

It felt almost as though they were begging me to follow them, that they expected something from me that I could not refuse to do. The Bai were famous for their hospitality. How kind they both were to make sure I found my way up challenging Cock's Foot and not get lost.

As the mother took the lead and the girl passed me by, I wondered for an instant if the package on her back was moving, but decided it was just my imagination. Maybe the higher altitudes were affecting me. After an hour or so of climbing, we arrived at their home, a simple wooden hut on a steep slope with a shaky verandah extending out the back, where the mother invited me to join her, her husband, daughter, and son-in-law for tea. They appeared all dressed up and as having gathered for a special event.

I was sipping my tea, enjoying the cool breezes, and chatting with my hosts. Suddenly, the young daughter started bowing before me. Her head bounced up and down to the floor, over and over again. She joined her hands as if in prayer. I had no idea what was going on but wondered if perhaps it was a form unknown to me of Bai hospitality.

All at once, the girl began rapidly unwrapping her shawl that was woven tightly around her back and shoulders. Out emerged a newborn baby boy!

"What is going on?" I asked in Chinese—trying to keep calm.

"We want you to name our baby," the Bai husband answered.

"Oh, yes, th—th—thank you very much," I stuttered," but I can't. I don't know a name for a Bai baby boy."

"Oh, but you must," everyone insisted in chorus.

The young mother started bowing vigorously again after laying her newborn wrapped in her shawl at my feet. She was breathing heavily. I was afraid she would faint. I stalled as long as I could while the family kept pressing me on. My elementary Bai language skills were not up to naming a Bai baby. Suddenly, in utter frustration, I cried out in Chinese, "*Guang-rong! Guang-rong!*" (光榮) "Glory Boy, Glory Boy."

The whole family was ecstatic. They danced around and around, joyously passing back and forth their precious "Glory Boy." I feared they would fall off their verandah, or their dancing would smash its flimsy construction.

I was excited as I took their photos so I could remember the Bai family's joy and a Bai mother's pride they had shared with me on Cock's Foot Mountain.

When I got back to Dali and shared my Bai naming event, a Bai anthropologist friend was ecstatic. "Congratulations!" he cried. "Now you are a full member of the Bai. And what a lucky child Glory Boy is. Right now, you should send him a pair of short pants to wear as a sign of your kinship with his Bai parents. When he grows up and goes to the United States to college, you must pay for his tuition!"

Was I being duped? Was this mysterious encounter somehow planned by the Bai? I will never know. It was a wondrous event. A marvelous sortie to bless a Bai newborn. I believe it was a pure experience devoid of deceit. Why? I was beginning to accept more and more the inexplicable. I felt like the weaver who was weaving a spiritual rug for me was tugging on a strand of wool more tightly. Plus Glory Boy never showed up at my American door for his college tuition.

A Tibetan Monk
Becomes My Didi, A Younger Brother

Icontinued my climb to the top third of Cock's Foot. The trail was somewhat tricky to follow, and in some steep places, arduous. There are now hundreds of well-built steps and even an electric trolley, but back then, I was fortunate to get to the peak without getting lost.

Five hundred feet from the summit, I made my way to a spacious outjutting platform of granite at the base of a towering cliff face. I set up a little altar on a low flat boulder. I laid my large red bandana on top as an altar cloth. Upon it, I placed my Daily Office prayerbook and a favorite unframed photo of a Chinese icon of the Virgin Mary, before whom I would now sit cross-legged and meditate upon my East-West Buddhist-Catholic pilgrimage thus far.

It was not long before a Tibetan monk, a lama dressed in a saffron robe suddenly emerged from some hidden opening in the cliff, bowed to the Virgin, smiled, and gestured a request to join me in prayer. I nodded, and he folded his legs and sat opposite me, chanting a sutra for a half-hour.

After some shared silence, he gestured to the Virgin with both palms joined, and bowed, knowingly.

I guessed he probably mistakenly thought Mary was the Buddhist Goddess of Mercy, the bodhisattva Avalokitesvara. She is known as Chenrezik in Tibet. Originally a male figure in India and Southwest Asia, she became feminine in East Asian cultures, known in China as Guanyin and Kannon in Japan. But the monk knew the figure my icon portrayed.

"She is the Virgin Mary, the Mother of Jesus," I said simply in Chinese, assuming he knew the language. He nodded fervently and drew a deep breath.

He touched the bottom hem of her long gown behind which her feet were hidden, and bowed tenderly. "I know, *Gege*," he said, honoring me by calling me "my elder brother" in Chinese.

"I met the Dalai Lama once," I murmured, somewhat breathlessly. "In a welcoming line during his visit to a local college." In hindsight, I realized I was nearly overwhelmed by this mystical nanosecond—the mysterious appearance of the lama, the fact that we were sitting together in homage to Mary at the face of Huashou Gate, where the historical Buddha's disciple experienced realization and awakening.

At the mention of the Dalai Lama, the monk gleamed, his face luminous with joy. He got up, sat cross-legged beside me, and reached into a hidden pocket in the fold of his robe. Then he carefully handed me a forbidden newspaper photo of the Dali Lama and Pope Paul VI at a private papal audience. We gazed at the picture together side-by-side for a long while in a space beneath the cliff, sacred to us both, basking in our newly found spiritual friendship.

Abruptly there came the sound of a voice—someone ascending the trail. The lama hastily tucked the Dalai Lama's image deep inside his secret pocket, stood up, bowed, and disappeared.[30]

I had known nothing of Cock's Foot Mountain's Buddhist ancestry, let alone that Tibetans were living there again after a hiatus of centuries. All I had wanted was to take a weekend break from my encounters with Bai oral tale-tellers and villagers. The mountain event of meeting the Tibetan monk felt heaven-sent, yet another providential meeting. There would be more for me to realize in knowing the meaning of these events, but a deepening intuition was unfolding within me.

The Babus in the Back Room
Indore, India

A few years after the sabbatical in Mysore, in 1996, I served with Bonnie for several months as a volunteer at a Mother Teresa refuge, Jyoti Nivas, "Residence of Light," in Devanāgarī (Indore), in the central state of Madhya Pradesh, India. Our assistance there was an "accident." Our plan had been for us to live in a newly forming interfaith ashram while I continued the work on Southern Silk Road folktales I had begun in Mysore. We resided at the ashram, although its inter-religious aspirations never got off the ground due to caste conflicts.

One day as we biked around Indore, we were amazed to discover a Mother Teresa hospice. Our finding it seemed serendipitous. Could we serve as volunteers in the hospice? To our surprise, the Mother Superior welcomed us.

When we returned to begin our volunteering, we visited the hospice chapel. There before us were two brief phrases pinned at opposite ends of the altar: "Abide in me" and "I thirst" (John 15: 4; 19:28). Jesus told his disciples that, if they were to bear fruit, they must remain in him as he remained in them, like branches on the vine. The second phrase was Jesus' saying on the Cross, as he cried out for a drink. These two phrases became my "India koan." How was I to rest in Jesus while witnessing the suffering at Jyoti Nivas?

Bonnie worked upstairs in the nursery and orphanage, where the little ones, infants, toddlers, school-age children, and high school girls fell in love with her and she with them. I happily joined her. There were wonderful compensations in volunteering. Often Bonnie and I set a mat down on the floor, and each of us would have a pile of babies crawling all over us. It was an utter joy to be covered by a half-dozen babies, sitting on our feet and legs and lap, or hanging from our necks.

Seven of Bonnie's Children

Five More

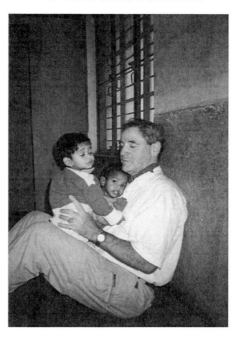

Lucien's Turn

My main role was to stand by destitute men from the streets downstairs, helping them—in Mother Teresa's words—"die like angels." I again awoke to a deeper identity with the Holy Innocents. My affinity with them had already taken hold through the spiritual seeds planted in me at Father Oshida's fire Mass at Takamori and in his union with the blood of Jesus and Mary in Mary's pregnant womb at Mary House. The photo of little Kim Phuc Phan Tri's running screaming towards me, her back burning with American napalm, the unforgettable fire we dropped on Hiroshima and Nagasaki, and the abortion of the unwanted unborn *kodomo* all haunted me. But in an entirely different sense, I was also haunted too by a profound joy in being once again with the poor and the pure of heart—God's chosen ones, the Holy Innocents.

At Jyoti Nivas, they gave me another "assignment." I would attend those I eventually nicknamed "the backroom *Babus*." *Babu* respectfully addresses an adult man or male child. The "backroom" was an abode that seemed for me to be "for those for whom there is no room," in a hidden corner of the sanctuary. Somehow I never asked, but I knew the Sisters were desperate for space—a host of souls were out there awaiting death. Almost daily, the Mother Superior traveled the streets and byways of Indore, bringing home to Jyoti Nivas the hopeless and dying rejected for assistance at hospitals and

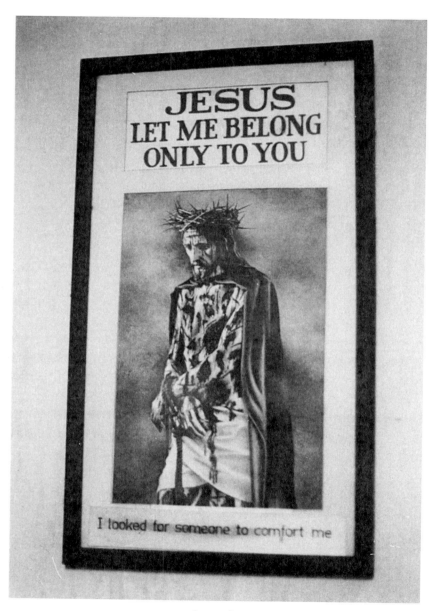

Author Photo

way-stations. The back room was small, cramped, dark, filthy, and somewhat creepy. When I arrived the first time by myself, I was greeted by feces and blood on the floor. There were three men on pallets, and three others on floor mats, their hand-held tin urinals alongside.

I remembered immediately my visit years previously to Mother Teresa's home convent in Kalighat. After morning Mass one day I wandered upstairs by myself to the laundry where the Sisters washed sheets, towels, clothing and diapers all by hand. I found myself alone that afternoon standing before a stunning portrait on the laundry walls of the flayed Jesus. I had never seen this image before: his scourged body crowned with thorns, his flesh torn open revealing bare sinews, his skin hanging in folds down his torso, arms and legs. At the top of the portrait was a prayer in bold letters: **"JESUS LET ME BELONG ONLY TO YOU."** At the bottom was the incomplete phrase from Psalm 69, "I looked for someone to comfort me," which the knowledgable worshipper mouths in silence, "but found none" (Psalm 69: 21). Again, my India koan. Belong to the flayed Jesus. Comfort the backroom Babus.

On one of my first days with the backroom Babus, I saw a nameless corpse in the corner. Covered with a muslin cloth, the body on the floor hosted a simple bouquet of dried flowers in a vase. One of the Babus had died, which of the six residents I did not know. I had yet to learn all their names.

The two I came to know best were Natur and Ramir. Both were dying, but Ramir, old, withered, and half-blind, was the worse off. When either one was uncomfortable, I would raise him to ease his pain. The first time I lifted Ramir, I saw under his body what I thought to be lice or flies' eggs, and flying insects hatching out. As I let him back down, I saw his urinal, an old plastic bottle, was filled. So I emptied it. He smiled as though he had seen Jesus.

I hurried home on my bike that day, submerged in Ramir's joy.

Kumar the Bold

On another occasion, when I visited the Babus, Natur's foot was bleeding profusely through a bandage. I ran to fetch one of the Sisters, and she hurried off to find "Kumar," a resident volunteer who she said was in charge of changing bandages.

Soon I heard a loud, rhythmic pounding, and someone swiftly approaching the backroom—"thump-thump-thump." It was one-legged Kumar swinging madly forward—with the panting Sister who had summoned him, a good ways behind—propelling himself forward on his distinctive single crutch—the rubber arm piece painted bright gold, and the wooden part, royal blue.

Kumar was stunningly handsome—thick, wavy, jet-black hair, a close-clipped mustache, long, crescent-shaped eyebrows arching over his eyes, and a trimmed, black, full beard. A twin to Laurence Olivier, a stand-in for Peter O'Toole, the star of *Lawrence of Arabia*. His dark, flashing eyes shone above his fulsome effusive smile that I soon learned was eternal. He was the surrogate doctor on call, a legend in his own time.

I nicknamed him, "Dr. Kumar." He loved it. (I also secretly called him "Saint Kumar," because he was a saint).

Kumar was holding his signature piece—a mint-green wooden shoe-box—at the ready for doctoring. He took care of all the men's needs in the most loving way. He cut hair and toenails, trimmed beards, gave shaves and haircuts, and dressed wounds. His shoebox was full of soap, razors, scissors, tape, gauze, bandages, and antiseptic, all mixed with his maintenance tools in the same do-it-yourself kit.

He did everything with a winning spirit of aplomb.

What Kumar gave was not so much a shave or the dressing of a wound, but a noble, loving presence, uplifting joy, and an illuminating smile that made the men he served so very happy.

I watched Kumar skillfully change the bandage. He stopped the bleeding, washed the wound, and poured an overly generous amount of antiseptic over it from a large bottle in his shoebox. Then Kumar proficiently wrapped a fresh bandage around the foot. He smiled the whole time and hummed a tune as he worked. While the men were delighted and comforted, I was not. Sterile conditions and simple hygiene were on my mind, obviously not on Kumar's.

To my shock and surprise, he next went about the room and kneeled on one leg beside each of the five wretched men, giving shaves and hair-cuts, all the while using the same unsanitary clippers, straight razor, and scissors he had been wielding all day.

Then with a bright smile and bow, Kumar left. After seeing Ramir's joy amidst his grief when I emptied his urinal, this experience of group therapy was a giant step forward for me on the koan trail—"abide and thirst."

The next day, I went looking for Kumar. Bonnie and I had brought sterilized bandages, rubber gloves, and face masks when we left home for Indore, anticipating a possible need like this one.

"Kumar," I said, "I have single-edged, disposable razors and face-masks to be used only once, and sterilized bandages." Francis, a resident of Portuguese descent who knew some English, translated. Kumar was in ecstasy, as he had been when he discovered an abandoned prosthesis after another resident had died, even though it could not replace his missing right leg, since it was for a left-footed amputee. When I pulled out each item, it was like Christmas back home with the children. Kumar grinned, nodded his head up and down in thanksgiving. His face shone like a rising full moon over these gifts from America. He was delighted to have these supplies and received each germ-free item with a dignified nod.

Two or three weeks later, when checking in on the group I called the "veranda gang" outside in their patio sitting in the sun, I saw face masks and pairs of rubber gloves stuffed into the meshes of an adjoining crown fence, waiting to dry. Kumar had hand-washed them in the patio's filthy dishpan. He alternated using each set on a different day of the week. He could not understand throwing something useful away. Wash it, dry it, save it. That way, with continued use, his Christmas gifts for serving the sick and dying would last forever.

Oh, For a Beedie!

The relief of the Babus in the Backroom was the sacred beedie—a poor man's cigarette—tobacco flakes wrapped in the leaf of the tendu tree and tied with string at one end.

Early on during my volunteer work, Natur had asked for a beedie, being heavily addicted. I fetched one from an invalid in the ward and lit it for him. He puffed away on his smoke in great, long ecstatic draughts. His companion on the floor-mat beside him, Ramir, blind in one upturned white eye, smelled the beedie smoke and signaled with two fingers to his lips that he wanted one too. So I fetched another.

Then I left the room, self-righteously denying the two smokers a second beedie.

After that, guilty over my lack of charity, each time I came to the home, I brought beedies for Natur, Ramir, and their neighbors.

During one of the next times I spent time with the Babus, I happened to have only one beedie on me, and knowing Natur's addiction, lit it and handed it to him. "No, for Uncle," he said and put the lit beedie between half-blind Ramir's lips who lay there moaning and shaking. It was an incredible act of generosity for the addicted Natur, a great renunciation that comforted his dying neighbor. Natur gazed lovingly into Ramir's one good eye, while Ramir nodded in gratitude. Natur reached out and patted Ramir on his wobbling knee.

"We are in this together," he seemed to be saying to his withering pal.

On my last visit to Jyoti Nivas, I found Natur and Ramir lying in the backroom as always. I had a fun plan in mind. It would be my going-away present to them, as it were, and to all the Babus who inevitably shared what little they had with one another.

When Natur signaled for his beedie, I gave him one as usual. When he beckoned me for a second beedie, knowing I would not give him one, I shocked him. I bent down, drew an entire pack of beedies from my shoulder bag, and slipped it into his shirt pocket. His face shone in the darkness. So did Ramir's when I gave him his. It was a moment of illumination for all the Babus in the Backroom, me most of all, when I saw their faces radiant with joy and gratitude.

"Matches?" My two Babus wondered aloud in a faint chorus. I added a box of matches to their shirt pockets. Both lay back on their pads in quiet ecstasy, waving their thanks. I told them tomorrow I was going to America. They understood this as my farewell.

"Namaste," they whispered tears in their eyes.

"Namaste," I answered.

I walked away in a flood of tears, knowing we were eternal friends.

For me, the "India koan" was solved. "Abide" and "Thirst" were one. In a rational sense, the koan remained an unfathomable mystery. But mystically "to abide" and "to thirst" were united in "Be Here Now," which was an existential awareness of the presence of God in a hands-on love of the suffering Holy Innocents. Serving with Bonnie at Jyoti Nivas, we felt the Hand of God.

At Jyoti Nivas in Indore, I felt God's pain and love through simple presence with the dying and those who love and serve them. In an epiphany of mystical joy, I found a resolution of my innocent suffering dilemma among "the Babus in the Backroom," my Mecca at the "Residence of Light." I understood my union with Fadi the Mysore market leper and his role of atonement at last in the sense that I had a taste of suffering that Mother Teresa called redemptive. Yet once again, we knew the discovery of Jyoti Nivas and our unexpected welcome to serve were gifts of the Spirit. In my wildest imagination, I never could have conjured up a poor house for the dying possessed with the riches of goodness and gratitude.

Thomas Merton's Quest for Wisdom

Seven years before his visit to Gal Vihara, Thomas Merton had written an exquisite mystical prose-poem on Holy Wisdom: *Hagia Sophia*.

> There is in all visible things an invisible fecundity, a dimmed light, a meek namelessness, a hidden wholeness. This mysterious Unity and Integrity is Wisdom, the Mother of all, *Natura naturans.*[31]

Over his twenty-seven years as a monk, Merton gradually came to realize that a comprehensive interfaith understanding of Wisdom was becoming a focal point of his monastic role and identity.

> I am more and more convinced that my job is to clarify something of the tradition that lives in me, and in which I live: the tradition of wisdom and spirit that is found not only in Western Christendom but in Orthodoxy, and also, at least analogously, in Asia and Islam.[32]

His quest was broad and comprehensive but also deeply personal. Merton's self-sense was that he experienced himself "as the object of Wisdom's friendship and intimate attention," notes Christopher Pramuk.[33] Object or not, Merton sought Wisdom until the end of his life. As Jonathan Montaldo wrote, Merton's journals give "hard evidence that he was unwise but in search of Wisdom. He was not already 'living with' Wisdom but following ancient ways for 'moving toward' Wisdom's house." He proposed that "Merton died a philosopher, one not yet wise but stumbling falteringly and passionately forward toward Wisdom."[34] We are much the poorer because Merton died before he could explore his Gal Vihara illumination in an East-West understanding of Wisdom.

Merton had divined Hagia Sophia's identity and qualities in his poem: invisible fecundity, dimmed light, a meek namelessness, hidden wholeness, mysterious unity, and integrity. These qualities might well describe Merton's experience with the Buddhist sculptures at Polonnaruwa. Something was unfolding at Gal Vihara for him. His vision became expansive as he gazed upon the motionless-momentum and light-heaviness of the stone figures of Buddha carved out of a rock cliff. In the silence and void of the surrounding valley, he encountered the twelfth century Sri Lankan Buddhist unveiling of ineffable mystery. The statues were aesthetically Buddhist but spiritually universal, a limped manifestation of Buddhist wisdom (*prajna*), the understanding of the true nature of phenomena, and invisible Sophia, the inner essence or uncreated ground and being of all things.[35]

Who or what is Sophia? When Merton first saw a painting by his artist-friend Victor Hammer of a young woman crowning the head of an adolescent Jesus, he recognized who she was. She was an all-inclusive image of an East-West "Lady Wisdom" whose reach stretched expansively from the Hebrew Scriptures to the nameless pivot of nature, Tao.[36]

My Awakening

I cannot explain my awakening at Jyoti Nivas with my beedie buddies Natur and Ramir. My sudden perceptions as I shared "time out of time" with my dearest Fadi the Leper and with Kumar the Bold remain a mystery, the meaning of my being with them abides out of my reach. My finger can only point to the moon. Like all the moments I have described in this brief account of my journeys in Asia, they felt for me like gifts of Wisdom with uncanny faint echoes of Merton's garden encounter at Gal Vihara in Polonnaruwa where he said:

> Looking at these figures I was suddenly, almost forcibly, jerked clean out of the habitual, half-tied vision of things, and an inner clearness, clarity, as if exploding from the rocks themselves, became evident and obvious.[37]

My memories of my time with the "holy innocents"—the marginal poor, sick, and dying like the "Napalm Girl," Parveeni the Star, the pure of heart like the Bai baby and the Tibetan lama—likewise reverberate within me when I read these lines. My vision of Thomas Merton's Lady Wisdom in Asia accords with the many who affirm it is She who penetrates the veil and unites all opposites and every contradiction, who beyond analytical cognitive understanding awaits us in all created things. Through my epiphanies in Asia, I found a manifestation of Christ among "the gentiles." I resolved my dilemma of failing to understand the suffering innocent by hanging out with "the Babus in the Backroom." These living sacraments of Holy Wisdom awoke my heart at last.

Author Photo

Epiphany at Polonarruwa

In 1995, Bonnie and I finally made our pilgrimage to Sri Lanka. Our experience was what Merton called "preverbal" and "post-verbal," qualities of an ineffable experience, beyond the level of words.[38]

Among the statues and ruins of Gal Vihara, we, at last, saw the other side of the mountain Merton had seen, the one he longed to see. What I remember vividly is Bonnie's and my quiet epiphany walking on the same holy ground of sand and grass as Merton had walked in 1968. We moved in bare feet, like him, as a pilgrim does in Asia visiting sacred locations, then sat silently that afternoon alone together contemplating the statues.

To our left was the fifteen-foot high sitting Buddha deep in meditation, *Dhyana*, perhaps at the juncture of enlightenment.

Author Photo

Before our eyes loomed the sculpture of the twenty-four foot high standing Buddha. His arms were crossed in the gesture of thanksgiving, probably evidence of his having achieved enlightenment after he had spent weeks gazing at the Bodhi Tree (sacred fig tree) in gratitude for having sheltered him. Many consider this one of the most notable of the Buddha's transcendent experiences in Asia.

Lying prone to our right lay the magnificent forty-six-foot long *parinirvana* Buddha at the juncture of his final extinction beyond the cycle of birth, death, and rebirth.[39]

Wiki Photo

Looking at the head and feet of the prone *parinirvana* Buddha at his moment of release, I saw Christ in the open tomb Holy Saturday, my most sacred day of the year.

Author Photos

My wife and I were alone in silent beauty. We had hoped to taste and see. We did.

Do I think these buddhas are God? No. Do I sense the stone statues are on to something, so to speak, pointing to and expressing it? Yes. Can I explain what it is? All I can say now is seeing and feeling them was a profound religious experience that brought me closer to the Word, Jesus, the Christ, the Second Person of the Blessed Trinity. I also sensed the presence of the feminine Wisdom of God. And I might add, the encounter brought me closer to the historical buddha, Gautama Buddha (Siddhārtha Gautama, Shakyamuni) as well.[40]

Perhaps my experience can be replicated for you should you care to meditate or pray before an image of the small clay statue of Jesus in the hands of Buddha which is placed close by Father Oshida's gravesite at Takamori. Many visitors say that seeing this statue in its sacred location is a religious experience. [41]

Heidimarie Kern sculpture
Photo Japanese Dominicans

The child Jesus is standing before his cross, his feet resting on the earth's globe that lies in the hands of Buddha. Jesus' hands and arms are extended, reaching out to us, inviting us to enter through him and his cross into the silence and stillness of the Buddha. My encounters with Gal Vihara, the Mysore market leper, and my beloved dying and destitute at Jyoti Nivas were manifestations of what I experience as "Jesus in the Hands of Buddha."

When I see this sculpture, it is as though the Buddha was basking in the Real Presence. My mind's eye sees the Amida Buddha of all-embracing love, his face radiating innocence and serenity, compassion and awareness, blissfully holding the Child Jesus in the mudra of deep contemplation, protecting and adoring the Child before the Cross, knowing full well who he is: Jesus, Son of Mary, Son of Man, Son of God, Word of God. And what he has done and what he will do: the heart of God in redemptive love and suffering on the Cross.

Perhaps if Thomas Merton had not died accidentally in Thailand, the day would have come when he realized that he had written himself out of this world. He would have transcended pilgrimage and disappeared from view, an apotheosis. Isn't that what he accomplished in Asia? Or rather, wasn't that what the Lord has done for him and us? Had the Lord made him invisible, in the mystical Body of Christ, lying among the stars (Phil. 2: 15)?

As for myself, I came to a new horizon, the resolution of the mysterious trajectories which haunted my Asian pilgrimage, the incidents of luck, chance, and destiny. Allow me to remember them with you:

> Here are my East-West masters of the contemplative life: Thomas Keating, Sasaki Roshi, William Johnston, Shigeto Oshida; the September Meeting with the poor who serve the poor; Jesus and Mary's pulse beating as one; the blasted ones, the girl-child Kim on fire with napalm, "Little Boy" the A-Bomb, the aborted kodomo; the Bai baby and Cock's-Foot Lama; the market leper, Babus, and Beedie Boys outback.

This cluster of happenstances turned out to be providential. Gradually I heard the voice of God, the *Bat Kol* calling me from the other side of the mountain: "Be there." Following my ordination to deacon in 1983 and return from Asia in 1993, my vocation became clear. I was called to sit with the holy innocents and pure of heart amid their sickness, isolation, or dying. My vocation was to become a companion as a spiritual director and walk with others seeking their true selves and their God whatever their faith may be. I have been summoned to "Hang out" so to speak with the Girl-Childs, the Fadis, Glory Boys, Kumars, Ramirs, and Naturs of the world. I believe my vocation to be present is a divine calling we all possess. Unlike me, may you not take years to answer it.

*The star that guided the Magi still burns with love
in the cosmos of the human heart.*[42]

Coda

URAKAMI MARY[43]
Photo Anne Martens

Oh Mary
Mother of the Holy Innocents
Born and unborn
Victims of slavery, genocide
War, abortion, and poverty
Who die at our hands
And redeem us in the Blood of the Lamb

Pray for us.

Scarred eyeless face exquisite
Beauty of the Virgin Survivor
You look upon us

With ultimate sorrow, understanding
Compassion and forgiveness.

In your voice we hear the prophets in prayer:

"Awake and sing, you who sleep in the earth,
for the dew of the Lord is a dew of light."

"They skip with joy like lambs, for you have set them free.
Earth resounds with the echo of their song."[44]

Notes

1. Thomas Merton, *The Asian Journal of Thomas Merton,* ed. Naomi Burton, Brother Patrick Hart, James Laughlin (New York: New Directions, 1973) 153.

2. For an intimate portrait of a providentially marked encounter with Christian-Buddhist spirituality, see my forthcoming book, *Jesus in the Hands of Buddha: A Lifelong Pilgrimage East and West.*

3. *The Asian Journal*, 233-236.

4. Raymond Brown, *The Birth of the Messiah* (New York: Doubleday, 1999) 350-351, 354-355. *Anawim:* The 'poor, humble, afflicted; the 'Poor Ones'. It came to refer more widely to those who could not trust in their own strength but had to rely in utter confidence upon God: the lowly, the poor, the sick, the downtrodden, the widows and the orphans.

5. Merton essay "The Time of the End is the time of No Room," *Raids on the Unspeakable* (New York: New Directions, 1964) 72-73.

6. *The Asian Journal*, 28.

7. See Lucien Miller, "Merton's *Chuang Tzu*," *Merton And The Tao: Dialogues with John Wu and the Ancient Sages,* ed. Cristóbal Serrán-Pagán y Fuentes (Louisville, KY: Fons Vitae, 2013) 51-61. Their view is echoed in the voice and writings of the late Jesuit pioneer in Christian-Buddhist encounter, William Johnston.

8. Lucien Miller, "The Thomas Merton—John C. H. Wu Letters: The Lord as Postman," *Merton And The Tao,* 159, 162, 168.

9. Father Johnston, mystical theologian, mystic and translator, and author of *The Mysticism of the Cloud of Unknowing, Christian-Zen, The Still Point,* and *Silent Music,* among other works, is widely honored for his studies of mysticism and for his major contributions to the development of Buddhist-Christian encounter in Japan. He died in 2010.

10. Pope Francis Homily, "Solemnity of Mary, Mother of God," (www.vatical.va., January 1, 2019).

11. Florence Moran Gillman, "Within the Word: Peter and Paul," *Give Us This Day*, (Collegeville, MN: June 28-30, 2020) 307.

12. Thomas Merton, "Lecture Notes on Theology and Mysticism," *Merton and Hesychasm* (Louisville, KY: Fons Vitae, 2003) 441. See: David Bradshaw, "The *Logoi* of Beings in Greek Patristic Thought," *Toward an Ecology of Transfiguration,* ed. John Chryssavgis, Bruce V. Foltz (New York: Fordham University Press, 2013) 9-13.

13. *holokleros.* Merton, "a man who has attained full maturity and integrity in spiritual life." *Lecture Notes on Theology and Mysticism* (Collegeville, MN: Liturgical Press, 2017) 439. St. Paul, "May the God of peace himself make you perfectly holy and may you entirely, spirit, soul, and body, be preserved blameless for the coming of our Lord Jesus Christ." *Thessalonians* 5: 23.

14. Chiemi Ishii, "Encounter with Takamori—Encounter with the Deep Stream," http://www.dominicos.telcris.com/en/encounter.htm. Chisato Kitagawa translation, email to Lucien Miller, March 17, 2017.

15. *Bat Kol* definitions from Jewish Encyclopedia.

16. An insight of my friend and writing mentor, Susan Solinsky.

17. Chisato Kitagawa translation from Oshida, *A Far Away Look (Tooi Manazashi)* 102, 105-106.

18. Chisato Kitagawa translation from Oshida, *Confession of a Fisherman (Ryooshi no Kokuhaku)*. Oshida refers to the story of the breakfast barbecue at the beach around which the disciples gathered with the Risen Christ in the Gospel of John 21: 1-119. The union of fire, the Holy Spirit, and the Eucharist is an ancient Christian teaching, most noted annually in the Easter fire which begins the liturgy of the Easter Vigil on Holy Saturday, representing Christ's resurrection. See Yves Congar, OP, *I Believe In The Holy Spirit* (New York: Seabury, 1983) for Holy Spirit and fire references in Ephrem of Syria, Isaac of Antioch, and others. In the office of Matins, the Second Sunday after Pentecost, we read: "Here is the body and blood which are a furnace in which the Holy Spirit is the fire."

19. Ishii, "Encounter."

20. September Conference references are from my personal notes and Chisato Kitagawa's translations of Japanese materials.

21. Vietnamese National Huynh Cong "Nick" Ut Photo, Associated Press. The American coordinator of the attack suffered PSD for years, but his guilt was assuaged when Kim forgave him during a Vietnam War Memorial gathering in Washington, D.C.

22. *Unforgettable Fire* (Tokyo, NHK, 1977). English translation (New York: Pantheon Books, 1981). Toshio Kanamitsu was the Chief Director of the NHK education department.

23. Chisato Kitagawa email to Lucien Miller, Dec 16, 2018.

24.Regarding this sacred moment, see Franciscan priest Richard Rohr's account in *Divine Dance: The Trinity and Your Transformation* (New Kensington, PA: Whitaker House, 2016) 53. Rohr's book advances a paradigm shift in our traditional understanding of the triune God, and face-to-face encounter with the Trinity.

25. *Divine Dance*, 86.

26. U. S. Catholic. Jan. 23, 2019.

27. Mother Teresa, *In the Heart of the World.* Ed. Becky Benenate (Novato, CA: New World Library, 1977). Mother Teresa, *Come Be My Light.* Ed. Brian Kolodiejchuk (New York: Doubleday, 2007). "Mother Teresa's Theology of Suffering," *Theology and the City.* March 16, 2012. https://theologyandthecity.com/2012/03/16/mother-teresas-theology.

28. Mother Teresa quotation source not identified. Quoted everywhere.

29. The combined population of minority groups comprise 8.49% of the population of mainland China.

30. Tibetans in Tibet live in a totalitarian police state. Public displays of devotion to the Dalai Lama or his picture are forbidden in the PRC, which terms him a "wolf in monk's robes." There are an estimated 6 million Tibetans in China.

31. Merton, "Hagia Sophia," *Emblems of a Season of Fury* (Norfolk, CT: New Directions, 1963) 61-69. "Hagia Sophia" was completed Spring, 1961, and originally published by Victor Hammer. (Lexington, KY: Stamperia del Santuccio, 1962). *"Natura naturans,"* "nature naturing," nature as self-generating, dynamic, and animate.

32. Merton, *Conjectures of a Guilty Bystander* (Garden City, NY: Dell, 1967) 194.

33. Christopher Pramuk, *Sophia: the Hidden Christ of Thomas* Merton (Collegeville, MN: Liturgical Press, 2009) 13. Here I shadow Christopher Pramuk's astonishing revelations

of Merton's discovery of Wisdom and the feminine divine in his *Sophia* and his equally brilliant *At Play In Creation: Merton's Awakening to the Feminine Divine* (Collegeville, MN: Liturgical Press).

34. Jonathan Montaldo, "A Testament of Confession and Witness," *The Merton Seasonal* (Louisville, KY: International Thomas Merton Society, Spring, 2020) Vol. 45, No. 1, 9 & 11.

35. David Bradshaw, "The *Logoi* of Beings in Greek Patristic Thought."

36. See Merton's May 2, 1959 letter to his friend, artist Victor Hammer, on the latter's copy of a drawing of Hagia Sophia, "Lady Wisdom," crowning the young man Jesus. Quoted in Susan McCaslin, "Merton and 'Hagia Sophia,'" in *Merton and Hesychasm, 235.*

37. *The Asian Journal, 235.*

38. *The Asian Journal*, 315.

39. For interpretations of the Buddhas see "Gal Vihara," Wikipedia. Solitary solitude in 1995 enhanced our Gal Vihara pilgrimage immensely, the foundation of wisdom as Alexander Lipski writes: "wisdom could only be attained following the practice of contemplation in solitude." *Thomas Merton and Asia* (Kalamazoo, MI: Cistercian Publications) 65. Today there are guards, hoards of foreign tourists, Sri Lanka students on field trips, roped off areas, and overhanging canopies protecting the statues but impairing vision and aesthetic and contemplative experience.

40. Also known as Siddhārtha Gautama, Shakyamuni Buddha.

41. Clay sculpture gift to Father Oshida by Heidimarie Kern, a German Catholic nurse who came to Japan to practice *zazen* under Yamada Koun Roshi (山田耕雲), visited Fr. Oshida and stayed several times at Takamori. Reprinted photo by her permission.

42. Father Guerric DeBona, OSB, "Nightlight," *Give Us This Day* (Liturgical Press: Collegeville, MN, January, 2020) 89.

43. Urakami Mary (Hibakusha or Nagasaki Mary) is the blackened bust of the full-length painted wooden Madonna miraculously discovered in the ashes of the Urakami Cathedral of the Immaculate Conception razed by the Nagasaki Atomic Bomb, cindering worshippers and priests inside, August 9, 1945. The cathedral was filled that day in anticipation of the Feast of the Assumption, August 15.

44. Isaiah 26: 19 & 21; Divine Office Feast Of The Holy Innocents, December 28.